DANTE'S *RIME*

THE LOCKERT LIBRARY OF POETRY IN TRANSLATION
Editorial Adviser, John Frederick Nims
For other titles in the Lockert Library, see page 267

DANTE'S *RIME*

TRANSLATED BY PATRICK S. DIEHL

Princeton University Press · Princeton, New Jersey

Published by Princeton University Press, Princeton, New Jersey
In the United Kingdom: Princeton University Press, Guildford, Surrey

Library of Congress Cataloging in Publication Data will be
found on the last printed page of this book

The Lockert Library of Poetry in Translation is supported by a
bequest from Lacy Lockert (1888-1974)

This book has been composed in linotype Granjon

Clothbound editions of Princeton University Press books are
printed on acid-free paper, and binding materials are chosen for
strength and durability.

Printed in the United States of America by
Princeton University Press, Princeton, New Jersey

CONTENTS

49057

INTRODUCTION

THE COLLECTION

These poems are the records of a great poet's achievement of his greatness. The earliest are juvenilia; the latest, products of Dante's full maturity. Among them, they span a quarter-century, the years from the early 1280s till 1308 or later which also saw the writing of the *Vita nuova*, the *De vulgari eloquentia*, and the *Convivio*. Their culmination is the *Divine Comedy*.

The collection as we have it is disorderly and heterogeneous, abandoned by its author to history. Yet, for the sake both of the light it casts upon the *Comedy* and of the masterpieces it contains, it has a claim upon our attention as great as do the works of a Virgil or a Milton written before the creation of their epics. Be cautioned, however, that there is no norm here to serve as benchmark; the very lack of any norm is the essential fact. From the beginning, Dante experimented restlessly, taking all the risks available and inventing new ones. The first sonnets (1-7) try out the style fashionable in his adolescence. It is a laboriously mannered style, and Dante had only harsh words in his later life for its chief exponent Guittone, but these gawky first attempts turn out to have been indispensable to the final synthesis. A fellow poet, Guido Cavalcanti, showed Dante the way to the next stage in his development, the creation of the *dolce stil novo* or "sweet new style." In full reaction against the grotesqueries of Guittonian verse, the two, along with their followers, made a poetic revolution. They banished political and moral themes in favor of an exclusive concentration upon love and its effects, simplified their diction radically, and avoided nearly all the traditional rhetorical figures so prevalent in Guittone, including even simile and metaphor. All this made for much greater directness and emotional force, and one can see its results in poems 8 through 68 here and of course in the *Vita nuova*, the unrivaled triumph of the new aesthetic. But it also made for a narrowness which shut out most of experience. The poems which Dante incorporated into the *Vita nuova* do not appear in this translation. I feel that they ought not to be read in isolation from the gloss with which their author welded them into a masterpiece. The reader can refer to one of the numerous English versions of the *Vita nuova* to find the poems omitted here. They are numbers 6, 10-12, 20, 24, 26-29, 33-37, 40, 42-44, and 46-57.

The rest of the collection (ca. 1295 on) shows Dante moving out beyond the confines of the *dolce stil novo*. Poems such as the moral *canzoni* 69 and 70 or the flyting with Forese Donati (72-74a) are entirely alien to it. The latest of the pre-exilic works (i.e., 1301 or earlier), the *rime petrose* ("stone poems" or "poems about Petra," 77-80), share the subject-matter of the *stil novo* period, but treat it quite differently; love is no longer compounded of light and air and clear refining fire, it has become a dark, devastating, obsessive passion. Number 80, the last in the set of four, gives full expression to the violence of Dante's feelings and stands among the greatest of medieval poems. The others in the set are more restrained and so less gripping, but they are scarcely less remarkable even so. In 77, each stanza handles the well-worn theme of "winter is here but I burn with love" from a different aspect—astronomical, meteorological, zoological, botanical, and geological—and this bravura display is rounded off by an exquisitely lyrical envoi. The lover's sufferings are in the foreground, and the lady herself is scarcely visible—there is only her impassive beauty at the back of the picture. Number 78 is a sestina in which the beloved is identified with

4

and dissolved into a series of views of one landscape. The form admirably reproduces the effects and movements of obsession with its reiterated key-words, but again the woman remains an archetypal, natural force, her body rock and grass, her glance the sun itself. The third poem (79) of the group raises the sestina to a higher power. The redoubled repetitions become incantatory; when the poem is read aloud, the form takes possession of the reader, and the key-words ring like struck metal. Critics generally describe this poem as an *étude transcendentale* in pure technique; Dante himself is defensive when he mentions it in the course of *De vulgari eloquentia*; yet I believe that because—not in spite—of its form, it has an elemental ritual force rare in our European grand tradition.

With no. 81, "Around my heart, as if they went to earth," we enter the period of Dante's exile. The subject of this poem, perhaps the very finest in the whole collection, is highly esoteric, yet Dante sees it in movingly human terms. Who else could have successfully presented the concepts of divine law, the unwritten law of humanity (*ius gentium*), and actual law and the theme of human transgressions against justice in the form of a conversation between Love and three outcast, wandering women? Perhaps Langland, but he lacked Dante's discipline and control. This *canzone* demonstrates what the medieval gift for seeing abstractions in concrete terms as a part of human life could achieve when given wings by extraordinary imagination and complete technical mastery.

The remaining poems, save for the very last (89), deal with moral themes (83 excels even 69 and 70) or the laws of Love (the sonnet exchange with Cino da Pistoia, 84a-88).[1] They are utterly confident, and at least one, the sonnet "I have

[1] Though pre-exilic, nos. 84 and 84a are part of the exchange, and Foster and Boyde have therefore violated chronological order to place them alongside their brother sonnets.

stood now in the brightness of Love's beams" (86), ranks among the finest of Dante's lyrics. (In general, Dante is at his best in the longer forms, and his sonnets are of minor importance, but there are occasional exceptions.) The *canzone* that ends the *Rime* makes a splendid farewell; it incorporates elements of all prior periods in its style and imagery, harking back to a view of love and the beloved that Dante had, for some years already, left behind. Whether intentionally or not, its envoi closes out the long years of experimentation very neatly.

Looking forward to the *Comedy* (which Dante may have already begun by this time) and backward over the *Rime*, we see that all the skills Dante had developed are comprehended in his *magnum opus*. Many of the women there speak pure *stil novo*. The fine-drawn metaphysics of *canzoni* like 59 are indispensable to the disquisitions in the *Purgatorio* and *Paradiso*. The moral passion of *canzoni* 69, 70, and 83 burns brightly in the indignant speeches of Cacciaguida and Peter Damiani and St. Peter and of the Narrator himself. Even the vigorous scurrility of the exchange with Forese Donati (72-74a) finds its proper place, in the grotesque cantos xxi-xxii of the *Inferno* and in the squabblings of the damned. Of course, there are features of the *Comedy* that appear nowhere in the *Rime*: the extended *similes*, the economical and vivid characterizations, and the *terza rima* form itself. Yet even these features, scarcely to be expected, after all, in non-narrative poetry, derive clearly from traits of imagination and technique already in evidence in the *Rime*.

Thus, if the reader's interest is primarily in Dante's development as it relates to the *Comedy* and if his stamina is beyond question, it would make excellent sense to begin at the beginning and read straight through to the end. But if he is looking primarily for outstanding poetry that is reasonably accessible, it would be best to begin with the *petrose* (77-80), go on to 81, and thence to nos. 89, 83, 70, 61, 67, and

6

69, in that order. Only then should he dip into the earlier poems. Dante plundered the output of his youth for the *Vita nuova*, and what remains to represent that period in the *Rime* is not likely to win many post-medieval hearts. Therefore, my advice is to read this book as if it were Chinese, from back to front.

MATTERS OF FORM

Those not acquainted with medieval Italian versification should find the ensuing section useful. For a more comprehensive treatment, in English, the reader may turn to Foster and Boyde's *Dante's Lyric Poetry*, volume I, pages xliv-lv (see Select Bibliography). Except for the sestina and double sestina (concerning which see my notes to nos. 77 and 78), there are only three forms with which we need concern ourselves: the sonnet, the ballata, and the canzone.

The sonnet-scheme Dante follows will probably be familiar to the reader in the guise of the so-called Petrarchan sonnet as practiced by Milton or Wordsworth, for instance. Variants such as an ABABABAB rhyme-scheme in the octave (rather than ABBAABBA), or a sestet on two rhymes instead of three, appear here and there. Among the earliest poems, there is even the "double" sonnet, in which four lines are intercalated in the octave, two in the sestet (such as 8, 10, and 12). Lines in Dante's sonnets are of the standard hendecasyllabic length (eleven syllables, with a mandatory stress on the tenth, and at least one caesura within the line); the form itself can be seen as a type of *canzone* stanza, though with crucial differences (see below). It serves as the vehicle for occasional poetry, especially for correspondence on questions of love-service, and also for concentrated treatment of serious subjects of a certain weight.

The *ballata* was in theory suitable for lighter moments only, but in Dante's hands it shows itself capable of greater things (as in 64). It is composed either of one stanza or of several identical stanzas introduced by a brief preparatory strophe like the burden of a carol. The stanzas fall into two parts, with the first subdivided once more; the two main parts of the stanza are linked by rhyme. The introductory strophe, or *ripresa*, gives the theme of the *ballata* and the length and rhyme-scheme of the second part of each stanza (see 21).

The canzone could be described as a *ballata* without its *ripresa*, each stanza ranging from ballata-length (seven to ten verses) up to twenty lines long. Usually, though not necessarily, the chosen stanza-form is repeated up to seven times, with different rhyme *sounds* in each stanza, but the same rhyme-*scheme* and the same pattern of line-lengths. Usually, the *canzone* is rounded off by an envoi (*congedo*), which may be identical with the second part of the other stanzas, independent in form, or another full stanza to itself. For illustration of its many uses, one need only look through the *canzoni* here translated (13, 25, 32, 59, 61, 68-70, 77, 80, 81, 83, and 89). The stanzas themselves derive from the still more elaborate contrivances of the troubadours during the past two centuries. Their structure can be either monolithic or bipartite, with either or both of the two parts further divided. As in the *ballata*, the break between the two major sections, if there is a break, will be bridged over by the rhyme-scheme (here the sonnet, where the break between octave and sestet is sharply defined, is in clear contrast). Generally, the lines in a *canzone*-stanza are either seven or eleven syllables long, with the former restricted in Dante's practice to not more than one per subdivision. In a single poem, 70, penta-syllables appear, along with internal rhyme, but this is exceptional. As for the rhyme-scheme, Dante scrupulously connects the subdivisions of his stanzas. For the close of a stanza, he prefers a forceful couplet, though usually without any pause in the sense to set it off from the rest of the stanza. In practice, the *canzone*-form is capable of an enormous variety of effects; in the *Rime*, nos. 59 and 70 give some notion of the range available. Its movement can be solemn and stately or brisk and aggressive; the only constant is its mass and complexity. Ben Jonson's "strict Pindarics" and Wordsworth's Immortality Ode provide an approximation in our own English tradition to the effect of the *canzone*, but even they are not quite the same. The *canzone* grew out of a tradition in which poets had themselves written the melody for their own texts. The very words *canzone* and *ballata* recall the origins of these forms in song and in dance. It is true that in Dante's time poets no longer set their own poems nor expected others to set them. But musical form survived in the structure of the stanza—witness the XXY, XYY, or XXYY construction, corresponding to the two melodies and their repetitions which we find in the music of the troubadours up to and including the relatively late Arnaut Daniel (d. ca. 1200), a poet particularly admired by Dante. English odes and pindarics, on the other hand, are an attempt at the distance of well over a millennium to revive a classical form once itself based on music, but without any real awareness of that lost music to undergird its revival. They can never have the naturalness and freedom that the canzone still possessed in Dante's time; it was a living form, not a resuscitation, and it did not become rigidified till after Petrarch.

Rhyme in Italian is usually disyllabic, though monosyllabic (*tronca*) and trisyllabic (*sdrucciola*) rhymes are not uncommon. In Dante, and in medieval poetry in general, one also encounters homonym rhyme (*equivoca*), composite rhyme (cf. Byron's "intellectual / hen-pecked you all"), and, very rarely, rhyme between two occurrences of the same word without any change of sense or syntactical function. The early sonnets provide the clearest instances of *rime composte*

9

(especially 3a and 4) and *equivoche*, but these also appear in later lyrics and in the *Comedy* itself, where whatever stylistic device best meets Dante's purpose is called into service.

Finally, Dante's rhythm seems exceptionally free, even for Italian. The interplay between caesuras, stresses, and word-lengths, augmented by enjambement, is rich and supple. Rarely will two lines with the same rhythm occur in succession, and then only for special effect (as in 16). Beside these subtleties, metrical English verse seems stiff.

ON TRANSLATING DANTE

In the *De vulgari eloquentia* (II.viii-xiv), the *Convivio*, and throughout his verse, Dante lays particular stress upon the formal aspects of poetry. I have followed suit, not only in constructing this introduction, but more important, in translating the *Rime*. Iambic has replaced syllabic meter, and feminine endings have been reduced to masculine; otherwise, Dante's rhyme-schemes and line-lengths have been faithfully reproduced, even in the sonnet exchanges, where the correspondents will deliberately choose the rarest and most difficult rhyme-sounds in order to make the task of duplicating them in the reply all the more arduous. Like nearly all great poets, Dante was a superlative technician; certain of his poems (no. 70 in particular) would crumble to dust if stripped of their formal virtuosities; all draw heavily upon telling rhymes and careful construction within each stanza for their effect. The translator must embrace the technical demands of his task as a magnificent opportunity; to flinch from them would be fatal to this poetry. The only liberty taken here is occasional slant-rhyming of the mildest possible sort.

To pursue such a course puts considerable pressure on English idiom and syntax, so long as one aims at reasonable lexical fidelity, as I have. The reader must judge how far I have succeeded in resisting this pressure. Certain subjunctive and conditional constructions no longer current appear intermittently and contribute to the suggestion of things past that I felt was necessary to maintain historical distance. I have tried to avoid the corrupting archaisms that seem to ease the task but spell the ruin of a translation; for instance, I have altogether excluded verb-object inversions (e.g., "I have no remedy *my wounds to heal*").

I have also sought to keep padding to a minimum. Nothing destroys the effectiveness of a verse more completely, or plagues more translations. The constant use of periphrasis is a direct reflection of the original; Dante's periphrases are not empty ones, and I hope that neither are mine. Occasionally, I have added a phrase, voluntarily, for interpretive reasons. For instance, the last six words of the first line of no. 81, "Around my heart, as if they went to earth" have no counterpart in the Italian. But the poem portrays Justice and her daughters as hunted animals, and it seemed right to have them seeking their burrow in the opening line. Likewise, "my scaffold" in the first line of 77 brings out what is latent in the poem as a whole. Dante describes himself as being in a condition of spiritual paralysis bordering on death; the macrocosm in all its aspects threatens to become his execution-ground, with heaven as the wheel on which he is broken.

At other points, I have diverged widely from the surface sense of the text in order to make its meaning clear. Sometimes Dante's contemporaries found him rather obscure; what was merely obscure to a fourteenth-century Italian reader will usually be opaque to a twentieth-century reader of English. To make my readers' task easier, I have moved a certain amount of material I discovered in the commentaries or puzzled out for myself up into the body of the text. Thus, no. 83, vv. 93-94, which translate "literally" as "I do not know, because that circle surrounds us which limits us from up there," becomes in my version "No one—the stars that hem us in prevent / Our rising to the light . . . ," which makes it clear that Dante is thinking of deterministic astrological influences. On similar grounds, at the end of 74a, I have replaced the millet seeds of the original with a more familiar but nonetheless contemporary counting-device, the abacus. By and large, it is probable that I ought to have done more of this, but period color and lexical fidelity have their claims as well. Nor should we forget that a perfectly accessible, lucid, easy Dante would be a falsification.

So far as rhythm is concerned, I have made no attempt at direct imitation of the effects Dante gets from his hendecasyllabics except in the matter of pauses in the sense and enjambement. What I have produced is fairly regular iambic verse seasoned with a number of inverted feet and clashes of stress. I hope that it catches the speed and energy of certain poems, the decorum and melodiousness of others. The main object, as I saw it, was to preserve a sense of movement *through* the stanza, with syntax dancing its own pattern within the patterns of rhyme and line-length. Local effects are less crucial, and often inimitable.

When all explanations have been made, the business of verse translation remains a perilous one. Rigorists anathematize it; among them is Dante himself, who writes in *Convivio* I.vii.14, "nothing which has been rendered harmonious through unifying musical means can be translated from its own tongue into another without destruction of all its sweetness and harmony." Scholars grumble at the lexical infidelities of translators committed in the name of fidelity to the manifold unity of all aspects of the poem or to the underlying meaning they perceive. Poets wince at the strained language and scrupulous obscurities to which translators are driven by their desire to preserve as much of the original as possible. Yet the enterprise continues. Rigorists are wrong to say that "all" the original is lost in transmission; the scholars

12

are wrong to ask that poetry play the role of a crib; the poets are wrong to expect the tang of native harvests in exotic hybrids. But translation is the art of compromise, and the pure in heart will never love her.

My own goal has been the creation of good, vital English verse that can stand by itself but that remains unobtrusively yet recognizably alien. In Dryden's terms, the results lie somewhat to the metaphrastic, or literal, side of paraphrase. They may serve to interest the reader in the original, or to convey some notion of what the original is like to those without Italian, or even to bring new insights to those already familiar with the original texts. Whatever the case, these are ultimately poems not by Dante but by the translator; to read Dante, one must read Italian. And yet—I think you will find Dante here, for all that!

CONCERNING THE TEXT AND NOTES

The text of the *Rime* that I am following and that is reprinted here is the same as the text printed in K. Foster and P. Boyde, *Dante's Lyric Poetry* (Oxford, 1967), volume I. In its turn, this is in all essentials but the order of the poems identical to the edition by Michele Barbi under the auspices of the Societa Dantesca Italiana (Florence, 1960, reprint of the 1921 edition). The poems written by hands other than Dante's are denoted by being printed in italics in the Italian versions, and by the letter *a* following the number of each poem. About half the poems can be dated with reasonable precision; the other half can only be placed within whatever group they seem to belong to. This means that the main lines of Dante's poetic growth are clearly drawn, but that one must be careful when bringing specific poems in evidence to support generalizations about stylistic changes.

My notes are based upon the admirable commentary contained in volume two of the Foster-Boyde edition of the *Rime*. For further information, and for prose assistance in reading the originals, one need only turn to their work.

In closing, I want to render thanks to Peter Whigham, without whose early encouragement I would never have attempted to go beyond the *petrose*; to Jim Powell and Bill Tuthill, members of my verse translation class at Berkeley, and more particularly to John Frederick Nims, for their criticisms which spurred me on to a thorough revision of these texts; and to the University of California, for research grants which helped defray the expenses attendant upon the preparation of the typescript.

THE *RIME*

1a   (DANTE DA MAIANO)

Provedi, saggio ad esta visïone,
e per mercé ne trai vera sentenza.
Dico: una donna di bella fazone,
di cu' el meo cor gradir molto s'agenza,

mi fé d'una ghirlanda donagione,
verde, fronzuta, con bella accoglienza:
appresso mi trovai per vestigione
camicia di suo dosso, a mia parvenza.

Allor di tanto, amico, mi francai,
che dolcemente presila abbracciare:
non si contese, ma ridea la bella.

Così ridendo, molto la baciai:
del più non dico, ché mi fé giurare.
E morta, ch'è mia madre, era con ella.

1a

Attend, O poet, to this dream of mine
And pray, extract its true significance,
As thus: a lady whom One had fashioned fine,
To do whose pleasure is pleasure in advance,

Gives me a wreath of blossom and of vine
Well-leafed and green, and shows no diffidence.
But feel! its coolness spilling down my spine,
A gown has clothed me—one of hers, I sense.

And then, dear friend, I make myself so bold
As take her gently into my embrace—
She does not struggle, lovely all in laughter.

And as she laughs, I kiss her times untold . . .
I'll say no more—I swore it to her face.
A woman, dead—my mother—followed after.

1

Savete giudicar vostra ragione,
o om che pregio di saver portate;
per che, vitando aver con voi quistione.
com so rispondo a le parole ornate.

Disio verace, u' rado fin si pone,
che mosse di valore o di bieltate,
imagina l'amica oppinïone
significasse il don che pria narrate.

Lo vestimento, aggiate vera spene
che fia, da lei cui desïate, amore;
e 'n ciò provide vostro spirto bene:

dico, pensando l'ovra sua d'allore.
La figura che già morta sorvene
è la fermezza ch'averà nel core.

1

You best expound the theme that you assign,
Your standing in the ranks of wit is high;
Avoiding all dispute lest you repine,
To choicest words I now attempt reply.

Unfeigned desire, which scarcely knows decline,
Which beauty moves or worth that will not die,
Such does your friend believe and here opine
The first gift that she gave must signify.

Hope, and be safe in hoping, by the clothes,
That she you seek will play a lover's part—
Herein, your dreaming spirit well foreknows

(This second gift, I read, was just the start.)
The figure which, already dead, arose
Is steadfastness that she will bear at heart.

2

Per pruova di saper com vale o quanto
lo mastro l'oro, adducelo a lo foco;
e, ciò faccendo, chiara e sa se poco,
amico, di pecunia vale o tanto.

Ed eo, per levar prova del meo canto,
l'adduco a voi, cui paragone voco
di ciascun c'have in canoscenza loco,
o che di pregio porti loda o vanto.

E chero a voi col meo canto più saggio
che mi deggiate il dol maggio d'Amore
qual'è, per vostra scienza, nominare:

e ciò non movo per quistioneggiare
(ché già inver voi so non avria valore),
ma per saver ciò ch'eo vaglio e varraggio.

2

The jeweller who would try his gold and know
Its worth, if any, makes fire and puts it in
And doing so, can tell, when it runs thin,
Whether its price, dear friend, be high or low.

And for appraisal of my wordy show
I come to you, the chief among that kin
Who make a dwelling-place of learning's inn
Or walk with praise wherever they may go.

With all the art I can, I sing my spell:
Say which of all the woes of Love would be
The worst—by all you know, tell me its guise;

I want to see (but let's not syllogize,
You're far too quick with arguments for me)
What I am worth, and if I promise well.

2a   (DANTE DA MAIANO)

Qual che voi siate, amico, vostro manto
di scienza parmi tal, che non è gioco;
sì che, per non saver, d'ira mi coco,
non che laudarvi, sodisfarvi tanto.

Sacciate ben (ch'io mi conosco alquanto)
che di saver ver voi ho men d'un moco,
né per via saggia come voi non voco,
così parete saggio in ciascun canto.

Poi piacevi saver lo meo coraggio,
e io 'l vi mostro di menzogna fore,
sì come quei ch'a saggio è 'l suo parlare:

certanamente a mia coscienza pare,
chi non è amato, s'elli è amadore,
che 'n cor porti dolor senza paraggio.

2a

Whatever be your name, dear friend, your throw
Of knowledge seems too high for me to win;
Indeed, from ignorance I'm all chagrin,
Too low to praise, to pay my debts too low.

Know and be certain (I've learned this must be so)
Next you I'm less in knowledge than a pin
Nor is it cloth of wisdom that I spin
While in each line your weight and wisdom show.

Since you have asked to hear what I've to tell,
I'll show you all my heart, unfeignedly,
Just as they ought who traffic with the wise—

This is the only answer, in my eyes:
"Whoever loves, and yet unloved is he,
In his sad heart is sorrow's nonpareil."

3

Lo vostro fermo dir fino ed orrato
approva ben ciò bon ch'om di voi parla,
ed ancor più, ch'ogni uom fora gravato
di vostra loda intera nominarla;

ché il vostro pregio in tal loco è poggiato,
che propiamente om nol poria contarla:
però qual vera loda al vostro stato
crede parlando dar, dico disparla.

Dite ch'amare e non essere amato
ène lo dol che più d'Amore dole,
e manti dicon che più v'ha dol maggio:

onde umil prego non vi sia disgrato
vostro saver che chiari ancor, se vole,
se 'l vero, o no, di ciò mi mostra saggio.

3

Your finished verses turned with mastery
Confirm the good name gossip gives you here
And more besides—indeed, a man who'd try
To reach your praises' end could not come near,

For your ascendant honor stands so high
No man can see the summit of it clear,
And he who hopes to raise you to the sky
Would fall so short, he'd almost seem to sneer.

You say, to love yet unbelovèd be
Is heaviest grief at which Love's lovers grieve,
Yet many say that other griefs excel:

Humbly I pray (let wrath not fall on me)
Your light of thought establish (by your leave)
Which thing is true, so far as you can tell.

3a   (DANTE DA MAIANO)

Non canoscendo, amico, vostro nomo,
donde che mova chi con meco parla,
conosco ben che scienz' à di gran nomo,
sì che di quanti saccio nessun par l'à:

ché si pò ben canoscere d'un omo,
ragionando, se ha senno, che ben par là;
conven poi voi laudar sanza far nomo,
è forte a lingua mia di ciò com parla.

Amico (certo sonde, acciò ch'amato
per amore aggio), sacci ben, chi ama,
se non è amato, lo maggior dol porta;

ché tal dolor ten sotto suo camato
tutti altri, e capo di ciascun si chiama:
da ciò ven quanta pena Amore porta.

3a

Nothing, dear friend, I find that here betrays
Your name or town, though written with such spirit.
Yet fame must hold such learning up for gaze—
Of all the wise, I've known no one to peer it.

A talker shows himself in what he says—
If he's a man of sense, he'll soon appear it.
It's right I undertake your nameless praise,
But weight's too great and tongue too weak to pier it.

Dear friend (that's certain, for I should understand
Love, having loved), be sure who loves indeed,
And yet's unloved, the greatest sorrow's his;

All other sorrows (this their mother) stand
Under her rod who holds them all in deed:
From her comes all the pain that Love knows his.

4

Lasso, lo dol che più mi dole e serra
è ringraziar, ben non sapendo como;
per me più saggio converriasi, como
vostro saver, ched ogni quistion serra.

Del dol, che manta gente dite serra,
è tal voler qual voi lor non ha como;
e 'l proprio sì disio saver dol, como
di ciò sovente, dico, essendo a serra.

Però pregh'eo ch'argomentiate, saggio,
d'autorità mostrando ciò che porta
di voi la 'mpresa, acciò che sia più chiara;

e poi parrà, parlando di ciò, chiara,
quale più chiarirem dol pena porta,
d'ello assegnando, amico, prov'e saggio.

4

Ah, pain I feel most keenly! how it grips!
To owe you thanks that far exceed my sway!
Wisdom like yours, not mine, should walk this way,
Triumphing everywhere it comes to grips.

That pain you say strikes many with its grippes
On your own spirit seems most of all to weigh.
Yet I would learn this torment's every way—
Time and again we find ourselves at grips.

Cite me authorities, O wisdom's well,
Whose reasonings prove why what you say so is,
And let it rise to perspicuity;

And when all's clear through our acuity,
We'll settle which pain can most call sorrow his,
By logic, and experience as well.

5a   (DANTE DA MAIANO)

Amor mi fa sì fedelmente amare
e sì distretto m'have en suo disire,
che solo un'ora non poria partire
lo core mëo da lo suo pensare.

D'Ovidio ciò mi son miso a provare
che disse per lo mal d'Amor guarire,
e ciò ver me non val mai che mentire;
per ch'eo mi rendo a sol merzé chiamare.

E ben conosco omai veracemente
che 'nverso Amor non val forza ned arte,
ingegno né leggenda ch'omo trovi,

mai che merzede ed esser sofferente
e ben servir: così n'have omo parte.
Provedi, amico saggio, se l'approvi.

5a

Love makes me love with such fidelity
And in such bonds of longing holds me pressed
That not one hour can I prevent my breast
From thinking what he thinks and just as he.

Ovid I tried who claimed a "Remedy"
For curing us whom Love has sore distressed
But found him as mendacious as the rest
And here consign myself to crying "Mercy!"

And now I know, and know it as a fact,
When Love's afield, trust not to strength or art
Or wit or words determined men pursue,

But patient mind and pity's word and act
And loyal service: so have we each our part.
Consider, learned friend, if this be true.

5

Savere e cortesia, ingegno ed arte,
nobilitate, bellezza e riccore,
fortezza e umiltate e largo core,
prodezza ed eccellenza, giunte e sparte,

este grazie e vertuti in onne parte
con lo piacer di lor vincono Amore:
una più ch'altra ben ha più valore
inverso lui, ma ciascuna n'ha parte.

Onde se voli, amico, che ti vaglia
vertute naturale od accidente,
con lealtà in piacer d'Amor l'adovra,

e non a contastar sua graziosa ovra:
ché nulla cosa gli è incontro possente,
volendo prender om con lui battaglia.

5

Our courtesy, our knowledge, wit, and art,
Nobility, fair shape, and worldly sway,
Open hand, great strength, an unassuming way,
Courage, high gifts, together or apart,

These graces, virtues, yes, in every part
By their delight bring Amor into play—
Some more, some less entice him to the fray,
But all avail with him, and have their part.

Then if you wish, dear friend, to make the best
Of strength that's native or knows the work of chance,
Let Love determine time for it and place

Rather than toil against his work of grace:
For nothing has the strength to meet his lance,
Though fools forget and put their own in rest.

7

Com più vi fere Amor co' suoi vincastri,
più li vi fate in ubidirlo presto,
ch'altro consiglio, ben lo vi protesto,
non vi si può già dar: chi vuol, l'incastri.

Poi, quando fie stagion, coi dolci impiastri
farà stornarvi ogni tormento agresto,
ché 'l mal d'Amor non è pesante il sesto
ver ch'è dolce lo ben. Dunque, ormai lastri

vostro cor lo cammin per seguitare
lo suo sommo poder, se v'ha sì punto
come dimostra 'l vostro buon trovare;

e non vi disvïate da lui punto,
ch'elli sol può tutt'allegrezza dare
e' suoi serventi meritare a punto.

7

When shepherd Love strikes hardest with his stave
Be quick to heed him, put away your tricks,
For other counsel (this I'd swear by Styx)
Is not to be had—but heed me and behave!

Then, when the time is right, with herbs that save
He'll end those pains that tears and sighing mix,
For Love's worst woe, however harsh, is six
Times less than joy, when pure, is sweet. Now, pave

Your broken heart a carriageway where goes
His unexampled power, if he's warred
You to such feats as your good making shows:

And keep as close to him as key to ward
For he alone can pluck joy where it grows
And give his men their seasonable reward.

8

Se Lippo amico se' tu che mi leggi,
davanti che proveggi
a le parole che dir ti prometto,
da parte di colui che mi t'ha scritto
in tua balia mi metto
e recoti salute quali eleggi.

Per tuo onor audir prego mi deggi
e con l'udir richeggi
ad ascoltar la mente e lo 'ntelletto:
io che m'appello umile sonetto,
davanti al tuo cospetto
vegno, perché al non caler [non] feggi.

Lo qual ti guido esta pulcella nuda,
che ven di dietro a me sì vergognosa,
ch'a torno gir non osa,
perch'ella non ha vesta in che si chiuda;

e priego il gentil cor che 'n te riposa
che la rivesta e tegnala per druda,
sì che sia conosciuda
e possa andar là 'vunque è disïosa.

8

If it's friend Lippo by whom I'm to be read,
Before your thoughts have sped
To words that I will utter in short space,
Behalf of him who sent me to this place
I'm wholly in your grace
And give such greeting as you would were said.

I pray your honor hear me on this head,
And to your ears be wed
Both mind and wits in listening to my case:
An humble sonnet I of lesser race
Come now before your face
Lest you deny a hearing, as I dread.

To you I bring a girl, her body bare,
Who walks behind so circumspect and shy
She (wrongly) shuns your eye,
For not a stitch of clothes has she to wear;

Let that kind heart you guide your actions by
Clothe her, I pray, and make her all your care
That she be known and dare
Go each and any place her wishes lie.

9

Lo meo servente core
vi raccomandi Amor, [che] vi l'ha dato,
e Merzé d'altro lato
di me vi rechi alcuna rimembranza;
   ché, del vostro valore
avanti ch'io mi sia guari allungato,
mi tien già confortato
di ritornar la mia dolce speranza.
   Deo, quanto fìe poca addimoranza,
secondo il mio parvente!
ché mi volge sovente
la mente per mirar vostra sembianza:
per che ne lo meo gire e addimorando,
gentil mia donna, a voi mi raccomando.

9

This my obedient heart
May Love commend, who gave you it as bride,
And Pity at his side
Request of you for me some souvenir,
    For even as I start
Journeying from you, where virtues all abide,
My soul is fortified
With pleasant hopes of soon returning here.
    Lord, how small a thing these miles appear!
Or so I seem to find
And often send my mind
Behind, and look, and always you are near:
And therefore I, my noble lady, do
Commend myself, till I return, to you.

13

La dispietata mente, che pur mira
di retro al tempo che se n'è andato,
da l'un dei lati mi combatte il core;
    e 'l disio amoroso, che mi tira
ver lo dolce paese c'ho lasciato,
d'altra part'è con la forza d'Amore;
    né dentro i' sento tanto di valore,
che lungiamente i' possa far difesa,
gentil madonna, se da voi non vene:
però, se a voi convene
ad iscampo di lui mai fare impresa,
piacciavi di mandar vostra salute,
che sia conforto de la sua virtute.

    Piacciavi, donna mia, non venir meno
a questo punto al cor che tanto v'ama,
poi sol da voi lo suo soccorso attende:
    ché buon signor già non ristringe freno
per soccorrer lo servo quando 'l chiama,
ché non pur lui, ma suo onor difende.
    E certo la sua doglia più m'incende,
quand'i' mi penso ben, donna, che vui
per man d'Amor là entro pinta sete:
così e voi dovete
vie maggiormente aver cura di lui;
ché que' da cui convien che 'l ben s'appari,
per l'imagine sua ne tien più cari.

    Se dir voleste, dolce mia speranza,
di dare indugio a quel ch'io vi domando,
sacciate che l'attender io non posso;
    ch'i' sono al fine de la mia possanza.

13

My unrelenting mind, all retrospects
Into that time of which I stand bereft,
Brings on the one side war against my heart;
   But keen love-longing, which elsewhere bent directs
Me toward the beloved country I have left,
With Love allied assaults the other part;
   Nor do I feel within such strength or art
I might much longer hope to make defense
Except, my noble lady, you proffer it.
And then, if you see fit
To bring relief to my beleaguered sense,
Your pleasure be to send me your regard,
For she can heal the city Love has marred.

   Please you, my lady, not deny a port
To heart that loving brought to such dismay,
Knowing that you alone could send him aid;
   No lord that's good has ever pulled up short
In helping liegemen calling from the fray,
Lest honor, and his servants, die betrayed.
   And at my heart I feel a keener blade
When I consider, lady, how that you
Hang there a painting the hand of Love has wrought,
And, half a hostage, ought
To guard my heart more dearly than you do,
For He from Whom all excellence derives,
Because His image, most dearly bought our lives.

   Were you to say, sweet hope, that you extend
Delay across the path of what I need,
Be sure of this, I waited all I could
   And long since stumbled to my tether's end.

E ciò conoscer voi dovete, quando
l'ultima speme a cercar mi son mosso:
   ché tutti incarchi sostenere a dosso
de' l'uomo infin al peso ch'è mortale,
prima che 'l suo maggiore amico provi,
poi non sa qual lo trovi:
e s'elli avven che li risponda male,
cosa non è che costi tanto cara,
ché morte n'ha più tosto e più amara.

   E voi pur sete quella ch'io più amo,
e che far mi potete maggior dono,
e 'n cui la mia speranza più riposa:
   che sol per voi servir la vita bramo,
e quelle cose che a voi onor sono
dimando e voglio; ogni altra m'è noiosa.
   Dar mi potete ciò ch'altri non m'osa,
ché 'l sì e 'l no di me in vostra mano
ha posto Amore; ond'io grande mi tegno.
La fede ch'eo v'assegno
muove dal portamento vostro umano;
ché ciascun che vi mira, in veritate
di fuor conosce che dentro è pietate.

   Dunque vostra salute omai si mova,
e vegna dentro al cor, che lei aspetta,
gentil madonna, come avete inteso:
   ma sappia che l'entrar di lui si trova
serrato forte da quella saetta
ch'Amor lanciò lo giorno ch'i' fui preso;
   per che l'entrare a tutt'altri è conteso,
fuor ch'a' messi d'Amor, ch'aprir lo sanno
per volontà de la vertù che 'l serra:

My plight would be the clearer if you'd heed
How one last hope has kept me on the road—
　For back should stoop and carry load on load
Up to the weight that crushes rib and spine
Before it seeks a friend, even its best,
Lest he should fail the test—
For if it chance he waver or decline,
Nothing I know more bitter can befall,
For death comes quickly then and full of gall.

　And you are she where Love puts all my sight
And in whose gift still greater boons remain
And by whose side my hope has found her lair;
　For serving you alone I ask for light,
And all that brings you honor and good fame
I seek and wish—no other could I bear.
　Yours is to give what others would not dare,
For both my "yes" and "no" in your right hand
Were set by Love, whence greatness comes to me.
My sworn fidelity
Was moved by how you move and understand,
For each that sees you (when was this denied?)
Knows from without that mercy lives inside.

　Then let your greeting start her journey now
And come where she's expected, to my heart,
As you, my noble lady, see its cure.
　But let her know, before she leaves you, how
My heart is locked securely with that dart
Which Love shot home the day he made me sure,
　And hence its door will be an armature
To all but Love's envoys, who know the key
Is that power's will who keeps our hearts in jail.

onde ne la mia guerra
la sua venuta mi sarebbe danno,
sed ella fosse sanza compagnia
de' messi del signor che m'ha in balia.

Canzone, il tuo cammin vuol esser corto:
ché tu sai ben che poco tempo omai
puote aver luogo quel per che tu vai.

Wherefore in my travail
Her coming now is loss and injury
Unless with those who check and who compel,
Envoys of his beneath whose keep I dwell.

My song, pick out the shortest way and best,
For you can see how little time remains
That he may live for whom you take these pains.

14

Non mi poriano già mai fare ammenda
del lor gran fallo gli occhi miei, sed elli
non s'accecasser, poi la Garisenda
torre miraro co' risguardi belli,

e non conobber quella (mal lor prenda!)
ch'è la maggior de la qual si favelli:
però ciascun di lor vòi che m'intenda
che già mai pace non farò con elli;

poi tanto furo, che ciò che sentire
doveano a ragion senza veduta,
non conobber vedendo; onde dolenti

son li miei spirti per lo lor fallire,
e dico ben, se 'l voler non mi muta,
ch'eo stesso li uccidrò que' scanoscenti!

14

Not now, no never now could they amend
Their heavy fault, these eyes of mine, except
By going blind, since on the Garisend
(Tower of pleasant sights) they looked, and slept,

And did not recognize (ill be their end!)
Her who has most renown where praise is kept:
Thus both of them have forced me to extend
No peace their way, no matter how they've wept.

Their crime was such, that what should be perccived
(It stands to reason) without the help of eyes,
Seeing, they did not see; so failing, they

Have left my spirits bitterly aggrieved
And I aver (unless my purpose dies)
These ignoramuses myself I'll slay.

15

Guido, i' vorrei che tu e Lapo ed io
fossimo presi per incantamento
e messi in un vasel, ch'ad ogni vento
per mare andasse al voler vostro e mio,

sì che fortuna od altro tempo rio
non ci potesse dare impedimento,
anzi, vivendo sempre in un talento,
di stare insieme crescesse 'l disio.

E monna Vanna e monna Lagia poi
con quella ch'è sul numer de le trenta
con noi ponesse il buono incantatore:

e quivi ragionar sempre d'amore,
e ciascuna di lor fosse contenta,
sì come i' credo che saremmo noi.

15

Guido, I wish that Lapo, you, and I
Were taken up by strong ensorcelment
And set in ship, whatever winds were sent,
Who'd go the way we chose (no matter why),

And no misfortune, no untimely sky
Might ever make an hour's impediment,
And our minds being always of one bent,
Desire of more increase in every eye.

And mistress Vanna and mistress Lagia then,
With her whose number's thirty of three score,
Merlin would bring us, he who brought us there,

And talk of love would be our only care,
And each would be content to ask no more,
Just as I'm certain we would be, we men.

15a   (GUIDO CAVALCANTI)

S'io fosse quelli che d'amor fu degno,
del qual non trovo sol che rimembranza,
e la donna tenesse altra sembianza,
assai mi piaceria siffatto legno.

E tu, che se' de l'amoroso regno
là onde di merzé nasce speranza,
riguarda se 'l mi' spirito ha pesanza:
ch'un prest' arcier di lui ha fatto segno

e tragge l'arco, che li tese Amore,
sì lietamente, che la sua persona
par che di gioco porti signoria.

Or odi maraviglia ch'el disia:
lo spirito fedito li perdona,
vedendo che li strugge il suo valore.

15a

If I were he whom Love once called his clerk
(Whose memory now is all I've left to show)
And my love's face the same as long ago,
I would be greatly pleased with such a barque;

But you whom he preserves within his ark
There where reward and hope of it both grow,
Look at the weight which makes my spirit slow:
A ready bowman takes it as his mark

And shoots a bow, whose stringing was Love's care,
So irrepressibly, that you would call
Him very lord in joy's imperium.

Now hear the marvel, to what desire has come:
My stricken spirit forgives this archer all,
And yet he wounds beyond what it can bear.

Sonar bracchetti, e cacciatori aizzare,
lepri levare, ed isgridar le genti,
e di guinzagli uscir veltri correnti,
per belle piagge volgere e imboccare,

assai credo che deggia dilettare
libero core e van d'intendimenti!
Ed io, fra gli amorosi pensamenti,
d'uno sono schernito in tale affare,

e dicemi esto motto per usanza:
'Or ecco leggiadria di gentil core,
per una sì selvaggia dilettanza

lasciar le donne e lor gaia sembianza!'
Allor, temendo non che senta Amore,
prendo vergogna, onde mi ven pesanza.

16

The brachets belling, the huntsmen egging on,
The hares in flight, the hunters in full cry,
The leashes slipped, the greyhounds dashing by
Filling their jaws on green hillsides at dawn—

No doubt at all, these feats of speed and brawn
Delight a heart that's free of Love; but I,
Heavy with Love, heavy with thoughts that sigh,
Am mocked by one who walks the forest lawn.

Again he speaks to me, this *badineur*:
"Behold, such gallantry in gentle heart!
For this rough sport and these unsocial brooks

Abandon woman and her sweet sidelong looks?"
And as I tremble lest Love be told my part,
Shame mounts my face, my heart grows heavier.

17

Volgete li occhi a veder chi mi tira,
per ch'i' non posso più venir con vui,
e onoratel, ché questi è colui
che per le gentil donne altrui martira.

La sua vertute, ch'ancide sanz'ira,
pregatel che mi laghi venir pui;
ed io vi dico, de li modi sui
cotanto intende quanto l'om sospira:

ch'elli m'è giunto fero ne la mente,
e pingevi una donna sì gentile,
che tutto mio valore a' piè le corre;

e fammi udire una voce sottile
che dice: 'Dunque vuo' tu per nëente
a li occhi tuoi sì bella donna tòrre?'

17

Turn round and see who keeps me on his chain,
Through whom I cannot share your company,
And give him honor still, for this is he
Who makes of gentle women others' pain.

And to his strength, dispassionate yet my bane,
Offer a prayer that it may enter me:
I tell you, such of Love will lovers see
And of Love's ways, as eyes have shed of rain.

Fiercely he seized my thoughts, and in them drew
The picture of a lady of such worth
That to her feet my strength entirely flies;

He makes me hear a voice too fine for earth
Which says, "And so, for less than nothing, you
Would drive so fair a woman from your eyes?"

18

Deh, ragioniamo insieme un poco, Amore,
e tra'mi d'ira, che mi fa pensare;
e se vuol l'un de l'altro dilettare,
trattiam di nostra donna omai, signore.

Certo il vïaggio ne parrà minore
prendendo un così dolze tranquillare,
e già mi par gioioso il ritornare,
audendo dire e dir di suo valore.

Or incomincia, Amor, ché si convene,
e moviti a far ciò ch'è la cagione
che ti dichini a farmi compagnia,

o vuol merzede o vuol tua cortesia;
ché la mia mente il mio penser dipone,
cotal disio de l'ascoltar mi vene.

18

Come, Love, let's talk together—I'll confess,
And you'll assuage the cares in which I burn,
And if we'd both give pleasure, turn and turn,
Our lady, Lord, 's the theme, and hoped success.

Surely the miles we cover will grow less
When draughts of peace are drawn at that sweet urn,
And even now I've joy of our return
Telling and hearing told her gentleness.

Then you begin, dear Love—it's you who ought—
Continue now what worked in such a mode
That you consent to bear me company,

Be it deserving or your courtesy—
For now I rest disburdened of care's load,
Such longing for your words has filled my thought.

19

Sonetto, se Meuccio t'è mostrato,
così tosto 'l saluta come 'l vedi,
e va' correndo e gittaliti a' piedi,
sì che tu paie bene accostumato.

E quando se' con lui un poco stato,
anche 'l risalutrai, non ti ricredi;
e poscia a l'ambasciata tua procedi,
ma fa' che 'l tragghe prima da un lato;

e di': 'Meuccio, que' che t'ama assai
de le sue gioie più care ti manda,
per accontarsi al tu' coraggio bono.'

Ma fa' che prenda per lo primo dono
questi tuo' frati, e a lor sì comanda
che stean con lui e qua non tornin mai.

19

My sonnet, if Meuccio's there to hear,
Give him our greeting the moment that you meet,
Run up to him, fall prostrate at his feet—
I wish your birth and breeding to be clear.

And when you've been a little with my dear,
Again salute him, let you not retreat,
Then to the words I've sent you to repeat,
But first take him aside, where no one's near,

And tell him: "He who loves you most of men
Transmits his deepest joys into your hand
That he may win the friendship of your heart."

Make certain that he takes this gift to start,
Your brother sonnets, and leave them my command—
They stay with him, and don't come back again.

Per una ghirlandetta
ch'io vidi, mi farà
sospirare ogni fiore.

   I' vidi a voi, donna, portare
ghirlandetta di fior gentile,
   e sovr'a lei vidi volare
un angiolel d'amore umile;
   e 'n suo cantar sottile
dicea: 'Chi mi vedrà
lauderà 'l mio signore.'

   Se io sarò là dove sia
Fioretta mia bella [a sentire],
   allor dirò la donna mia
che port' in testa i miei sospire.
   Ma per crescer disire
mïa donna verrà
coronata da Amore.

   Le parolette mie novelle,
che di fiori fatto han ballata,
   per leggiadria ci hanno tolt'elle
una vesta ch'altrui fu data:
   però siate pregata,
qual uom la canterà,
che li facciate onore.

21

For a garland I
Saw, no flower here
But makes me sigh.

Lady, one time I saw you wore
A wreath of flowers of sweetest scent
  And over it an angel soar,
An angel boy, that Love had sent;
  And veiling his intent
He sang, "Who sees me near
Will praise my master's eye."

If I am ever where she is,
My fair and noble Fioret,
  Then will I tell my lady this—
She wears my sighs upon her head.
  But, that desire be fed,
My lady will appear
Crowned with Love's garlandry.

These tender words of mine, half-grown,
Flowers adance upon the air,
  Took to adorn them for their own
A dress another was to wear:
  So honor, at my prayer,
Whatever voice you hear
Lifting these verses high.

22

Madonna, quel signor che voi portate
ne gli occhi, tal che vince ogni possanza,
mi dona sicuranza
che voi sarete amica di pietate;
   però che là dov'ei fa dimoranza,
ed ha in compagnia molta beltate,
tragge tutta bontate
a sé, come principio c'ha possanza.
   Ond'io conforto sempre mia speranza,
la qual è stata tanto combattuta,
che sarebbe perduta,
se non fosse che Amore
contro ogni avversità le dà valore
   con la sua vista e con la rimembranza
del dolce loco e del soave fiore
che di novo colore
cerchiò la mente mia,
merzé di vostra grande cortesia.

22

My lady dear, that mighty lord your eyes
Are harbor to, to whom all bend the knee,
Is my security
That in your heart the house of pity lies;
  For where he wills his dwelling-place to be
The greatest beauties round about him rise,
And to him comes as prize
All good, for he is source and sovereignty—
  Whence I can solace hope that solaced me,
She who was long and sorely battle-tossed
And had been wholly lost
If love had lacked the power
To give me strength against this bitter shower
Through sight of him and by the memory
Of that dear place and the enchanting flower
Whose colors, new that hour,
Have ringed my spirit round,
Thanks to that courtesy with which you are crowned.

Deh, Vïoletta, che in ombra d'Amore
ne gli occhi miei sì subito apparisti,
aggi pietà del cor che tu feristi,
che spera in te e disïando more.

Tu, Vïoletta, in forma più che umana,
foco mettesti dentro in la mia mente
col tuo piacer ch'io vidi;
   poi con atto di spirito cocente
creasti speme, che in parte mi sana
là dove tu mi ridi.
   Deh, non guardare perché a lei mi fidi,
ma drizza li occhi al gran disio che m'arde,
ché mille donne già per esser tarde
sentiron pena de l'altrui dolore.

23

Ah Violet, in shade where Love reclines
Who rose without a warning on my sight,
Pity the heart which felt your weapons bite,
Which hopes in you and with desiring pines.

  Yours, Violet, a form that must be art
Put to the torch and sword my thoughtful tower
With only what I see,
  And then by act of all-enkindling power
Created hope which medicined that part
There where your smile struck me.
  Why wonder that I live confidingly?
Lift eyes to that desire in which I blaze,
Since thousand women now for their delays
Suffer the grief their lovers' pain assigns.

25

Lo doloroso amor che mi conduce
a fin di morte per piacer di quella
che lo mio cor solea tener gioioso,
   m'ha tolto e toglie ciascun dì la luce
che avëan li occhi miei di tale stella,
che non credea di lei mai star doglioso:
   e 'l colpo suo c'ho portato nascoso,
omai si scopre per soverchia pena,
la qual nasce del foco
che m'ha tratto di gioco,
sì ch'altro mai che male io non aspetto;
e 'l viver mio (omai esser de' poco)
fin a la morte mia sospira e dice:
'Per quella moro c'ha nome Beatrice.'

   Quel dolce nome, che mi fa il cor agro,
tutte fïate ch'i' lo vedrò scritto
mi farà nuovo ogni dolor ch'io sento;
   e de la doglia diverrò sì magro
de la persona, e 'l viso tanto afflitto,
che qual mi vederà n'avrà pavento.
   E allor non trarrà sì poco vento
che non mi meni, sì ch'io cadrò freddo;
e per tal verrò morto,
e 'l dolor sarà scorto
con l'anima che sen girà sì trista;
e sempre mai con lei starà ricolto,
ricordando la gio' del dolce viso,
a che nïente par lo paradiso.

25

That grievous love which brought me here tonight
Under the wings of death to pleasure her
Who used to make me feel joy was my home
   Has robbed and robs me daily of the light
My eyes conceived and held of such a star
I thought no grief could come where it had shone;
   And that deep wound which I have never shown
Is now discovered through excessive woe
Engendered by the flame
Which took me as its game
Till I have only suffering to expect;
And what life's left (how little must remain!)
Sighs as my death approaches, saying this:
"I die for her whom they call Beatrice."

   That too-sweet name, which is my heart's disease,
Each time they write it out and I look on,
Will make all sorrow new I suffer from,
   And in my grief I'll grow as lean as trees
That grew too fast, my face so woebegone
That fear strikes him who looks upon me dumb.
   And then no wind however slight will come
That does not kill, so that I topple cold;
And so I will be dead
With sorrow at my head
Beside my soul which takes her leave in gloom;
Henceforth they'll walk inalterably wed
Recalling joys they knew from those sweet eyes
Next whom there's nothing tempts in paradise.

Pensando a quel che d'Amore ho provato,
l'anima mia non chiede altro diletto,
né il penar non cura il quale attende:
   ché, poi che 'l corpo sarà consumato,
se n'anderà l'amor che m'ha sì stretto
con lei a Quel ch'ogni ragione intende;
   e se del suo peccar pace no i rende,
partirassi col tormentar ch'è degna;
sì che non ne paventa,
e starà tanto attenta
d'imaginar colei per cui s'è mossa,
che nulla pena avrà ched ella senta;
sì che, se 'n questo mondo io l'ho perduto,
Amor ne l'altro men darà trebuto.

   Morte, che fai piacere a questa donna,
per pietà, innanzi che tu mi discigli,
va' da lei, fatti dire
perché m'avvien che la luce di quigli
che mi fan tristo, mi sia così tolta:
se per altrui ella fosse ricolta,
falmi sentire, e trarra'mi d'errore,
e assai finirò con men dolore.

Thinking of all which Love and she have wrought,
My soul will ask no further last delight
Nor heed those pains the underworld appoints;
    For when my body wears itself to naught,
Love will go forth, whose bonds I find so tight,
With her to Him who judges our accounts;
    And if He grants no pardon to her crimes,
She will descend to torments she has earned
But does not cringe before,
And there will quite ignore
All but that image which made her break with life,
Feeling no pain that walks on that dark shore;
And though I lose all in this world of men,
Love in the other will pay me back again.

    Death, you who do the pleasure of that lady,
In pity, lord, before you take your prize,
Go up to her and ask
How it should chance the light of those fair eyes
Which bring such woe is wholly lost to me;
If someone else receives it presently,
Bring me the news and cancel my mistake,
And with less grief I'll celebrate my wake.

De gli occhi de la mia donna si move
un lume sì gentil, che dove appare
si veggion cose ch'uom non può ritrare
per loro altezza e per lor esser nove:

e de' suoi razzi sovra 'l meo cor piove
tanta paura, che mi fa tremare,
e dicer: 'Qui non voglio mai tornare';
ma poscia perdo tutte le mie prove,

e tornomi colà dov'io son vinto,
riconfortando gli occhi päurusi,
che sentier prima questo gran valore.

Quando son giunto, lasso, ed e' son chiusi;
lo disio che li mena quivi è stinto:
però proveggia a lo mio stato Amore.

30

From my dear lady's eyes there shines a light
So nobly lit, that where that light has been
Things are revealed that none could ever pen,
So new their being and so great their height;

And in her radiance my heart has gone dead-white
With fear, such fear I tremble in my den
And say, quite firm, "I'll not come there again"—
But no resolves endure against her sight

And so I turn back to my sure defeat
Telling my eyes, "Be brave" (all this, for what?
They knew at once her strength is absolute—)

And when I'm there, alas, they shudder shut,
Desire which drove them on has lost its heat.
Then be it Love who sees to his recruit!

31

Ne le man vostre, gentil donna mia,
raccomando lo spirito che more:
e' se ne va sì dolente, ch'Amore
lo mira con pietà, che 'l manda via.

Voi lo legaste alla sua signoria,
sì che non ebbe poi alcun valore
di poter lui chiamar se non: 'Signore,
qualunque vuoi di me, quel vo' che sia.'

Io so che a voi ogni torto dispiace:
però la morte, che non ho servita,
molto più m'entra ne lo core amara.

Gentil mia donna, mentre ho de la vita,
per tal ch'io mora consolato in pace,
vi piaccia a gli occhi mei non esser cara.

31

Into your hands, my lady gently bred,
I here commend my spirit as it dies,
Stumbling beneath such grief that from Love's eyes
(Who bids it go) some pitying tears are shed.

You set your heel so firmly on its head,
It had no power left for other cries
Than this: "My lord, whatever be the guise,
Whatever goal, I follow where I'm led."

I know you love no wrong—thought, done, or told—
And therefore death, an unjust, wrongful death,
Enters more bitterly my heart's sad room.

My noble lady, while I still draw breath,
That I may die in peace, and die consoled,
Do not begrudge my eyes your face's boon.

E' m'incresce di me sì duramente,
ch'altrettanto di doglia
mi reca la pietà quanto 'l martiro,
   lasso, però che dolorosamente
sento contro mia voglia
raccoglier l'aire del sezza' sospiro
   entro 'n quel cor che i belli occhi feriro
quando li aperse Amor con le sue mani
per conducermi al tempo che mi sface.
Oïmè, quanto piani,
soavi e dolci ver me si levaro,
quand'elli incominciaro
la morte mia, che tanto mi dispiace,
dicendo: 'Nostro lume porta pace!'

   'Noi darem pace al core, a voi diletto',
diceano a li occhi miei
quei de la bella donna alcuna volta;
   ma poi che sepper di loro intelletto
che per forza di lei
m'era la mente già ben tutta tolta,
   con le insegne d'Amor dieder la volta;
sì che la lor vittorïosa vista
poi non si vide pur una fïata:
ond'è rimasa trista
l'anima mia che n'attendea conforto,
e ora quasi morto
vede lo core a cui era sposata,
e partir la convene innamorata.

Of self-compassion now I bear such weight
Its torment surely will
Rival my martyrdom in groans and cries,
  Alas, and therefore, grieving at my fate,
I feel against my will
The gathering of my final, broken sighs
  Within my heart, which saw her lovely eyes
Strike when the hand of Love had found their key
To bring me to this season of distress.
Ah me, the modesty,
The innocence with which they seemed to look
That day they undertook
My own sole death, which takes me piece by piece,
And spoke these words: "Our vision carries peace."

  "Peace will we give your heart, and you, delight,"
They told my eyes at length,
Those that my lady wore from time to time;
  But when sure comprehension held their sight
That by her native strength
They had the rule and seisin of my mind,
  They turned and marched away with Love's ensign,
And glimpse of their all-conquering glorious trains
Forever to this conquest was denied:
Whence in her gloom remains
My soul which hoped she might be comforted.
My heart is almost dead,
The heart to whom she hitherto was bride
Yet she loves on though she must leave its side.

Innamorata se ne va piangendo
fora di questa vita
la sconsolata, ché la caccia Amore.
  Ella si move quinci sì dolendo,
ch'anzi la sua partita
l'ascolta con pietate il suo fattore.
  Ristretta s'è entro il mezzo del core
con quella vita che rimane spenta
solo in quel punto ch'ella si va via;
e ivi si lamenta
d'Amor, che fuor d'esto mondo la caccia;
e spessamente abbraccia
li spiriti che piangon tuttavia,
però che perdon la lor compagnia.

  L'imagine di questa donna siede
su ne la mente ancora,
là 've la pose quei che fu sua guida;
  e non le pesa del mal ch'ella vede,
anzi, vie più bella ora
che mai e vie più lieta par che rida;
  e alza li occhi micidiali, e grida
sopra colei che piange il suo partire:
'Vanne, misera, fuor, vattene omai!'
Questo grida il desire
che mi combatte così come sole,
avvegna che men dole,
però che 'l mio sentire è meno assai
ed è più presso al terminar de' guai.

  Lo giorno che costei nel mondo venne,
secondo che si trova
nel libro de la mente che vien meno,
  la mia persona pargola sostenne
una passïon nova,

Possessed by love she moves with tears upon
Her face toward her life's close
Disconsolate, for Love drives her apart.
   She looks as though all but her grief were gone,
And He before she goes
Hears her with pity Who made her by His art.
   Thus pent she lives in prison of this heart
With that poor life which shall be wholly spent
At my last hour when she abandons me,
And there makes her lament
To Love, who shut the world's door in her face;
And in a sad embrace
Her spirit holds her weeping constantly,
For soon division ends their company.

   The likeness of that lady keeps its throne
Undimmed behind my brow,
There where he set her (he who was her guide),
   And does not think the ills it views its own
But far more lovely now
Than ever, far more joyous, laughs inside,
   And lifts its eyes, and speaks, all homicide,
Proudly to her who weeps that she must flee:
"Be off, you beggar, out, this moment, go!"
So speaks my beloved to me,
Inflicting, as she always did, distress,
Although I feel it less,
For sense began to fail me long ago
And every day stands nearer end of woe.

   The day that she was sent into this world,
If truth is what is shown
In memory's book that fades as I handle it,
   My infant self, yet ignorant, uncurled
To passion then unknown,

tal ch'io rimasi di paura pieno;
   ch'a tutte mie virtù fu posto un freno
subitamente, sì ch'io caddi in terra,
per una luce che nel cuor percosse:
e se 'l libro non erra,
lo spirito maggior tremò sì forte,
che parve ben che morte
per lui in questo mondo giunta fosse:
ma or ne incresce a Quei che questo mosse.

   Quando m'apparve poi la gran biltate
che sì mi fa dolere,
donne gentili a cu' i' ho parlato,
   quella virtù che ha più nobilitate,
mirando nel piacere,
s'accorse ben che 'l suo male era nato;
   e conobbe 'l disio ch'era creato
per lo mirare intento ch'ella fece;
sì che piangendo disse a l'altre poi:
'Qui giugnerà, in vece
d'una ch'io vidi, la bella figura,
che già mi fa paura;
che sarà donna sopra tutte noi,
tosto che fia piacer de li occhi suoi.'

   Io ho parlato a voi, giovani donne,
che avete li occhi di bellezze ornati
e la mente d'amor vinta e pensosa,
perché raccomandati
vi sian li detti miei ovunque sono:
e 'nnanzi a voi perdono
la morte mia a quella bella cosa
che me n'ha colpa e mai non fu pietosa.

Such that I felt fear fill me every whit
    And on my powers fasten rein and bit
So unexpectedly, I fell to earth
Struck to my heart by light I could not bear.
And if the book has worth,
So great a trembling knew my vital breath,
I well believed its death
Had come into this world when she came there;
But pity held Him then Who made the air.

    When I beheld that form of loveliness
Which makes me weep apace,
(Mark you, good ladies, to whom may this be borne)
    That noble power than which all else are less,
While looking in her face,
Perceived that his destruction had been born
    And knew desire had caught him on its thorn
By that fixed gaze he bent upon her head—
Wherefore in tears he called his fellows home:
"You'll soon see here, instead
Of her I saw, a lovely imagery
Whose terror grows in me,
For she will have our scepter, crown, and throne
Soon as her eyes be pleased to take their own."

I chose to speak to you, my youthful ladies
Whose eyes are beauty's richest ornament,
Whose minds walk bound and pensive in Love's band,
That all the words I've sent
Commend themselves to you no matter where,
And I do here declare,
I pardon death I take at that fair hand
Whose is the blame and whence all pity's banned.

Onde venite voi così pensose?
Ditemel, s'a voi piace, in cortesia,
ch'i' ho dottanza che la donna mia
non vi faccia tornar così dogliose.

Deh, gentil donne, non siate sdegnose,
né di ristare alquanto in questa via
e dire al doloroso che disia
udir de la sua donna alquante cose,

avvegna che gravoso m'è l'udire:
sì m'ha in tutto Amor da sé scacciato,
ch'ogni suo atto mi trae a ferire.

Guardate bene s'i' son consumato,
ch'ogni mio spirto comincia a fuggire,
se da voi, donne, non son confortato.

38

Why do you walk with faces full of pain?
Please answer, in courtesy, if you'll stay,
For I'm afraid my lady (here's dismay)
Is why grief leads you hither in his train.

Ah, noble women, spare me your disdain,
Nor grudge my suit a pause along the way,
And speak to him who grieves and hopes he may
Learn somewhat of his lady, loss or gain.

Though it be hard to bear, yet I must know;
Love drove me out so often that I fled,
And now his every gesture seems a blow.

Consider this, that I am nearly dead
And that my powers will begin to go,
Ladies, unless you see I'm comforted.

Voi, donne, che pietoso atto mostrate,
chi è esta donna che giace sì venta?
sarebbe quella ch'è nel mio cor penta?
Deh, s'ella è dessa, più non mel celate.

Ben ha le sue sembianze sì cambiate,
e la figura sua mi par sì spenta,
ch'al mio parere ella non rappresenta
quella che fa parer l'altre beate.

'Se nostra donna conoscer non pòi,
ch'è sì conquisa, non mi par gran fatto,
però che quel medesmo avvenne a noi.

Ma se tu mirerai il gentil atto
de li occhi suoi, conosceraila poi:
non pianger più, tu se' già tutto sfatto.'

39

You ladies who wear pity as your dress,
Who is that lady lying where you leant?
She on whose image my whole heart's intent?
Ah, if it be, spare me no word, confess.

Her looks have changed, her loveliness is less,
That face which lay among you seems so spent
I know that it could never represent
Her face who was all women's blessedness.

"If you had doubts at first this was our lady,
So prostrate now, you need make no defense,
For you have done no other than did we;

But if you see the noble eloquence
Her eyes still have, you'll know that it is she;
Lament no more; you were undone long since."

41

Un dì si venne a me Malinconia
e disse: 'Io voglio un poco stare teco';
e parve a me ch'ella menasse seco
Dolore e Ira per sua compagnia.

E io le dissi: 'Partiti, va' via';
ed ella mi rispose come un greco:
e ragionando a grande agio meco,
guardai e vidi Amore, che venia

vestito di novo d'un drappo nero,
e nel suo capo portava un cappello;
e certo lacrimava pur di vero.

Ed eo li dissi: 'Che hai, cattivello?'
Ed el rispose: 'Eo ho guai e pensero,
ché nostra donna mor, dolce fratello.'

41

Mistress Dejection came to me one day
And sitting down, said this: "I've come to bide."
And as it seemed, she brought on either side
Sorrow and Gloom as comrades for the stay.

And I replied, "Get up and go away,"
And she gave answer with a Grecian's pride;
And as she talked, all manners cast aside,
I looked and saw lord Love who came our way

Attired in new-cut cloth as black as sloe
And with a cypress wreath upon his head,
And down his cheeks the tears were in full flow;

I called to him, "Poor prince, what has mis-sped?"
And he replied, "I walk with grief and woe—
Dear brother, our lady, she is nearly dead."

45

Di donne io vidi una gentile schiera
questo Ognissanti prossimo passato,
e una ne venia quasi imprimiera,
veggendosi l'Amor dal destro lato.

De gli occhi suoi gittava una lumera,
la qual parea un spirito infiammato;
e i' ebbi tanto ardir, ch'in la sua cera
guarda', [e vidi] un angiol figurato.

A chi era degno donava salute
co gli atti suoi quella benigna e piana,
e 'mpiva 'l core a ciascun di vertute.

Credo che de lo ciel fosse soprana,
e venne in terra per nostra salute:
là 'nd'è beata chi l'è prossimana.

45

Ladies I saw who made a noble band
Last All Saints' Day, I could not tell you where,
And one, as if their queen, was in command
And Love upon her right, and both were fair.

Her eyes poured forth such light on either hand,
It seemed a spirit made of fire and air,
And I was so emboldened that I scanned
Her face, and saw an angel figured there.

Kindly and gentle, according her salute
To all whom she judged worthy (as these were),
She filled each heart with virtue to the root.

In heaven few, I think, were mightier,
And she has come to save us at God's suit:
Blessèd is every woman close to her.

Per quella via che la bellezza corre
quando a svegliare Amor va ne la mente,
passa Lisetta baldanzosamente,
come colei che mi si crede tòrre.

E quando è giunta a piè di quella torre
che s'apre quando l'anima acconsente,
odesi voce dir subitamente:
'Volgiti, bella donna, e non ti porre:

però che dentro un'altra donna siede,
la qual di signoria chiese la verga
tosto che giunse, e Amor glile diede.'

Quando Lisetta accommiatar si vede
da quella parte dove Amore alberga,
tutta dipinta di vergogna riede.

58

By that way which Beauty runs alone
To waken Love by wakening thought in me,
Lisetta prances in her certainty
That she's the one who'll take me for her own.

And as she comes beneath that wall of stone
Which opens when both mind and soul agree,
She hears a voice address her suddenly:
"Fair lady, leave, and seek some other home;

Within this place another's chatelaine
Who had the rod of office fall to her
When she arrived, for Love supports her reign."

And when Lisetta heard dismissal came
From that same place where Love's a sojourner,
She came back hither blushing in her shame.

Voi che 'ntendendo il terzo ciel movete,
udite il ragionar ch'è nel mio core,
ch'io nol so dire altrui, sì mi par novo.
  El ciel che segue lo vostro valore,
gentili creature che voi sete,
mi tragge ne lo stato ov'io mi trovo.
  Onde 'l parlar de la vita ch'io provo,
par che si drizzi degnamente a vui:
però vi priego che lo mi 'ntendiate.
Io vi dirò del cor la novitate,
come l'anima trista piange in lui,
e come un spirto contra lei favella,
che vien pe' raggi de la vostra stella.

  Suol esser vita de lo cor dolente
un soave penser, che se ne gìa
molte fïate a' piè del nostro Sire,
  ove una donna glorïar vedia,
di cui parlava me sì dolcemente
che l'anima dicea: 'Io men vo' gire.'
  Or apparisce chi lo fa fuggire
e segnoreggia me di tal virtute,
che 'l cor ne trema che di fuori appare.
Questi mi face una donna guardare,
e dice: 'Chi veder vuol la salute,
faccia che li occhi d'esta donna miri,
sed e' non teme angoscia di sospiri.'

  Trova contraro tal che lo distrugge
l'umil pensero, che parlar mi sole
d'un'angela che 'n cielo è coronata.

59

You through whose knowing moves the heavens' third sphere,
Hearken to words the heart within me breeds,
For I can tell none else, my theme's so new.
    That sphere which follows where your power leads,
You noble creatures who attend me here,
Has brought me to that state I never knew.
    So this is fittingly addressed to you,
Speech of the life which holds me here apart:
I pray you now, heed what my words reveal.
I'll tell you all that's new and strange I feel,
How my sad soul is weeping in my heart,
And how a spirit bests her at Love's war
Who comes in light which travels from your star.

    My sorrowing heart had found its life before
In one beloved thought, which took his way
These many times up to our Lord's own seat,
    Where he beheld a lady bright as day,
Of whom his words delivered such sweet lore,
My soul would ask, "Might I kneel at those feet?"
    Now one is here he's fled from in defeat
And who has bound me with the strength of seven,
That my heart's fear is clear for all to trace.
He makes me look into a lady's face
And says: "You who would see the bliss of heaven,
Lift up your gaze, here, look into her eyes—
If you can bear an agony of sighs."

    He meets a foe that leaves his valor dead,
That humble thought which used to talk to me
Of a bright angel heaven crowned with light.

L'anima piange, sì ancor len dole,
e dice: 'Oh lassa a me, come si fugge
questo piatoso che m'ha consolata!'
   De li occhi miei dice questa affannata:
'Qual ora fu, che tal donna li vide!
e perché non credeano a me di lei?
Io dicea: "Ben ne li occhi di costei
de' star colui che le mie pari ancide!"
E non mi valse ch'io ne fossi accorta
che non mirasser tal, ch'io ne son morta.'

   'Tu non se' morta, ma se' ismarrita,
anima nostra, che sì ti lamenti,'
dice uno spiritel d'amor gentile;
   'ché quella bella donna che tu senti,
ha transmutata in tanto la tua vita,
che n'hai paura, sì se' fatta vile!
   Mira quant'ell'è pietosa e umile,
saggia e cortese ne la sua grandezza,
e pensa di chiamarla donna, omai!
Ché se tu non t'inganni, tu vedrai
di sì alti miracoli adornezza,
che tu dirai: "Amor, segnor verace,
ecco l'ancella tua; fa' che ti piace." '

   Canzone, io credo che saranno radi
color che tua ragione intendan bene,
tanto la parli faticosa e forte.
Onde, se per ventura elli addivene
che tu dinanzi da persone vadi
che non ti paian d'essa bene accorte,
allor ti priego che ti riconforte,
dicendo lor, diletta mia novella:
'Ponete mente almen com'io son bella!'

My soul is weeping still in grief that he
Is gone, and says, "Alas, how he has fled,
Kind thought which brought me comfort in the night!"
  And in her torment cries against my sight:
"Unhappy day that such a woman came!
Eyes, did you think I didn't know her well?
I said, 'Truly in those two eyes must dwell
He who will bring the likes of me our bane!'
To no avail that I was wide awake,
For still they looked—my thread of life must break."

  "You are not broken, only in dismay,
Dear soul of ours, whose grieving is so keen,"
A spirit said, whose love was plain to see,
  "For that fair woman whom you know as queen
Has so transformed your life from its old way
You are afraid, you walk so tremulously!
  Look at her kindness and humility,
How wise her greatness and how courteous,
And call her lady, yes, from this time on!
For if you keep the road, you'll see a dawn
Of beauties so augustly marvellous
That you will say: 'Love, my true lord and guest,
Behold your handmaid—do what you think best.'"

  My song, I fear there will be very few
To trace the path of meaning in your dance,
So hard the steps, so intricate the thought.
And if by any fortune it should chance
That people on the way encounter you
Who understand less fully than they ought,
Take heart, I pray, remember what I've taught,
And say, my new belovèd, as you can:
"At least you see how beautiful I am!"

60

Voi che savete ragionar d'Amore,
udite la ballata mia pietosa,
che parla d'una donna disdegnosa,
la qual m'ha tolto il cor per suo valore.

   Tanto disdegna qualunque la mira,
che fa chinare gli occhi di paura,
   però che intorno a' suoi sempre si gira
d'ogni crudelitate una pintura;
   ma dentro portan la dolze figura
ch'a l'anima gentil fa dir: 'Merzede!',
sì vertüosa, che quando si vede,
trae li sospiri altrui fora del core.

   Par ch'ella dica: 'Io non sarò umile
verso d'alcun che ne li occhi mi guardi,
   ch'io ci porto entro quel segnor gentile
che m'ha fatto sentir de li suoi dardi.'
   E certo i' credo che così li guardi
per vederli per sé quando le piace,
a quella guisa retta donna face
quando si mira per volere onore.

   Io non ispero che mai per pietate
degnasse di guardare un poco altrui,
   così è fera donna in sua bieltate
questa che sente Amor ne gli occhi sui.
   Ma quanto vuol nasconda e guardi lui,
ch'io non veggia talor tanta salute;
però che i miei disiri avran vertute
contra 'l disdegno che mi dà tremore.

Who talk of Love and know what you should say,
Listen to this ballata of my pain
Which tells you of a lady and disdain
Who by their power stole my heart away.

   With such disdain she greets whoever stares,
His eyes must turn away in sudden fear,
   For round about her own she always wears
The form of cruelty depicted clear;
   Yet in their depths a tender shape is near
Which draws from noble souls, "Be kind to me!"
And such its strength for all who look and see,
Their hearts must yield and give their sighs free play.

   I think she says, "I will not bow my head
Before those men who lift their eyes to mine,
   For at these gates that noble lord who sped
His darts into my soul has left his sign."
   I'm sure she guards her eyes with this design,
That she may look upon them at her will,
Just as good women use their mirrors till
They know they look as they should look today.

   I have no hope that pity ever could
Move her to glance elsewhere for all our sighs,
   So in her beauty is she fierce womanhood
Who feels how Love inhabits in her eyes.
   But let her keep him safe against surprise,
Deny me bliss, grant no unguarded hour—
No less for that will my desire have power
Against disdain which shakes me with dismay.

Amor che ne la mente mi ragiona
de la mia donna disïosamente,
move cose di lei meco sovente,
che lo 'ntelletto sovr'esse disvia.
 Lo suo parlar sì dolcemente sona,
che l'anima ch'ascolta e che lo sente
dice: 'Oh me lassa, ch'io non son possente
di dir quel ch'odo de la donna mia!'
 E certo e' mi conven lasciare in pria,
s'io vo' trattar di quel ch'odo di lei,
ciò che lo mio intelletto non comprende;
e di quel che s'intende
gran parte, perché dirlo non savrei.
Però, se le mie rime avran difetto
ch'entreran ne la loda di costei,
di ciò si biasmi il debole intelletto
e 'l parlar nostro, che non ha valore
di ritrar tutto ciò che dice Amore.

 Non vede il sol, che tutto 'l mondo gira,
cosa tanto gentil, quanto in quell'ora
che luce ne la parte ove dimora
la donna, di cui dire Amor mi face.
 Ogni Intelletto di là su la mira,
e quella gente che qui s'innamora
ne' lor pensieri la truovano ancora,
quando Amor fa sentir de la sua pace.
 Suo esser tanto a Quei che lel dà piace,
che 'nfonde sempre in lei la sua vertute
oltre 'l dimando di nostra natura.

Love, who commands the chambers of my mind
Discoursing of my lady passionately,
From hour to hour speaks things of her to me
At which my intellect bids me demur.
  Sweetly his words make music of such kind
My soul, which hears and feels how they agree,
Exclaims, "Alas, that I can never be
Equal to saying all I hear of her!"
  Before all else, surely I must defer
(If I would treat of what I hear him speak)
All that my intellect will never span,
And of that which it can
The greater part, because my tongue's too weak:
Wherefore, if rhymes I set to praise her name
Fall short of that perfection which I seek,
My halting intellect must bear the blame
And my frail words, that lack the strength or skill
To number pages Love would have them fill.

  The sun beholds, who circles all our sky,
Nothing so noble as when he turns his face
Disclosing light upon that happy place
My lady dwells, of whom Love makes me write.
  Each Intellect regards her from on high,
And those below who walk in Love's own grace
Find thoughts of her maintain their former space
Though Love has brought them all the peace he might.
  She pleases Him so much Who makes her bright,
He fills her with His power to her heart's brim,
More than our nature needs to play its role.

La sua anima pura,
che riceve da lui questa salute,
lo manifesta in quel ch'ella conduce:
ché 'n sue bellezze son cose vedute
che li occhi di color dov'ella luce
ne mandan messi al cor pien di desiri,
che prendon aire e diventan sospiri.

In lei discende la virtù divina
sì come face in angelo che 'l vede;
e qual donna gentil questo non crede,
vada con lei e miri li atti sui.
Quivi dov'ella parla, si dichina
un spirito da ciel, che reca fede
come l'alto valor ch'ella possiede
è oltre quel che si conviene a nui.
Li atti soavi ch'ella mostra altrui
vanno chiamando Amor ciascuno a prova
in quella voce che lo fa sentire.
Di costei si può dire:
gentile è in donna ciò che in lei si trova,
e bello è tanto quanto lei simiglia.
E puossi dir che 'l suo aspetto giova
a consentir ciò che par maraviglia;
onde la nostra fede è aiutata:
però fu tal da etterno ordinata.

Cose appariscon ne lo suo aspetto
che mostran de' piacer di Paradiso,
dico ne li occhi e nel suo dolce riso,
che le vi reca Amor com'a suo loco.
Elle soverchian lo nostro intelletto,
come raggio di sole un frale viso:
e perch'io non le posso mirar fiso,
mi conven contentar di dirne poco.

Her pure and virgin soul
Which takes that bliss of excellence from Him
Shows it in that which knows her government:
She bears such loveliness in heart and limb,
Heartward they send, they where her light is bent,
Runners who carry longing from their eyes
And turn to air and rise again as sighs.

On her, divine perfection shines as clear
As on an angel standing at His throne:
Let noble ladies who find this overblown
Attend on her and mark all that she does.
And when she speaks, I know I see and hear
One sent from heaven by whom all doubts are shown
How that high power which she contains alone
Surpasses all that nature grants to us.
Those acts of grace in which she's glorious
Call upon Love, each louder than the rest,
In such a voice he'll not lie long abed.
Of her it may be said,
Noble in woman is all that's in her breast
And lovely what resembles her the most.
And we can say her aspect helps us best
Accept what seems a wonder or a boast;
Hence faith is brought that succor which we need;
Before the world this woman was decreed.

Such things appear within her fair aspect
As show they bear the joys of paradise,
I mean, both in her smile and in her eyes,
Where Love brings them as if he brought them home.
Their strength has overcome my intellect
Like sight the sun has taken by surprise,
And since I flinch when I behold them rise,
I must content myself with what I've shown.

Sua bieltà piove fiammelle di foco,
animate d'un spirito gentile
ch'è creatore d'ogni pensier bono;
e rompon come trono
l'innati vizii che fanno altrui vile.
Però qual donna sente sua bieltate
biasmar per non parer queta e umile,
miri costei ch'è essemplo d'umiltate!
Questa è colei ch'umilia ogni perverso:
costei pensò chi mosse l'universo.

Canzone, e' par che tu parli contraro
al dir d'una sorella che tu hai;
ché questa donna, che tanto umil fai,
ella la chiama fera e disdegnosa.
Tu sai che 'l ciel sempr'è lucente e chiaro,
e quanto in sé non si turba già mai;
ma li nostri occhi per cagioni assai
chiaman la stella talor tenebrosa.
Così, quand'ella la chiama orgogliosa,
non considera lei secondo il vero,
ma pur secondo quel ch'a lei parea:
ché l'anima temea,
e teme ancora, sì che mi par fero
quantunqu'io veggio là 'v'ella mi senta.
Così ti scusa, se ti fa mestero;
e quando pòi, a lei ti rappresenta:
dirai: 'Madonna, s'ello v'è a grato,
io parlerò di voi in ciascun lato.'

Her beauty showers flamelets from her throne,
Enkindled by a spirit nobly born
Through whom arises every thought that's good—
As lightning shatters wood,
They break those inborn knots which bring us scorn.
Wherefore, that woman who hears her beauty blamed
For seeming boldly and unhumbly worn,
Follow her steps whence humbleness was framed!
It's she that humbles all who choose the worse
And was His thought Who formed the universe.

My song, I fear it seems you would belie
The claims a sister poem already made—
For that same lady you call a humble maid
She calls both fierce and full of harsh disdain.
You know that brightness always holds the sky
And in itself its light can never fade;
But our weak sight, by some appearance swayed,
Will say the very stars are on the wane.
Thus, when your sister calls our lady vain,
She does not see her as she really is
But as appearance makes her seem to be:
For fear has conquered me
And rules me yet, whence all is robbed of bliss
That I behold where her two eyes hold sway.
If you must ask for pardon, ask with this;
And when you can, present yourself, and say,
"My lady, if your pleasure bids me so,
I'll speak of you wherever I may go."

Parole mie che per lo mondo siete,
voi che nasceste poi ch'io cominciai
a dir per quella donna in cui errai:
'Voi che 'ntendendo il terzo ciel movete',

andatevene a lei, che la sapete,
chiamando sì ch'ell'oda i vostri guai;
ditele: 'Noi siam vostre, ed unquemai
più che noi siamo non ci vederete.'

Con lei non state, ché non v'è Amore;
ma gite a torno in abito dolente
a guisa de le vostre antiche sore.

Quando trovate donna di valore,
gittatelevi a' piedi umilemente,
dicendo: 'A voi dovem noi fare onore.'

62

My words that people speak of far and near,
You who were born the selfsame hour I came
To write of her whom I have sought in vain
"You through whose knowing moves the heavens' third sphere,"

Go now to her, who's known you many a year,
Calling out so, that she will hear your pain,
And tell her, "We are yours, and will remain
No more in number than you see us here."

Stay not with her, for Love left long ago,
But journey on in clothes that grief would wear,
For all your older sisters journeyed so.

And when a lady's found whose worth's not low,
Fall prostrate at her feet, and tell her there,
"To you be all the honor that we know."

O dolci rime che parlando andate
de la donna gentil che l'altre onora,
a voi verrà, se non è giunto ancora,
un che direte: 'Questi è nostro frate.'

Io vi scongiuro che non l'ascoltiate,
per quel signor che le donne innamora,
ché ne la sua sentenzia non dimora
cosa che amica sia di veritate.

E se voi foste per le sue parole
mosse a venire inver la donna vostra,
non v'arrestate, ma venite a lei.

Dite: 'Madonna, la venuta nostra
è per raccomandarvi un che si dole,
dicendo: "Ov'è 'l disio de li occhi miei?"'

63

O tender poems who talk both far and near
Of her whose worth ennobled womankind,
One's with you now, or can't be far behind,
Whom you'll receive, and say, "Our brother's here."

I conjure all of you, deny him ear
By that lord's name that lights a woman's mind,
For in his soul and body you will find
No word nor thought nor deed that holds truth dear.

But if from what he said a longing grew
To come where she your lady still receives,
Do not hold back: go up, and bow your head,

And say, "My lady, we have come to you
On his behalf who sits at home and grieves
Saying, 'Desire of my eyes, where have you fled?'"

'I' mi son pargoletta bella e nova,
che son venuta per mostrare altrui
de le bellezze del loco ond'io fui.

    I' fui del cielo, e tornerovvi ancora
per dar de la mia luce altrui diletto;
    e chi mi vede e non se ne innamora
d'amor non averà mai intelletto,
    ché non mi fu in piacer alcun disdetto
quando natura mi chiese a Colui
che volle, donne, accompagnarmi a vui.

    Ciascuna stella ne li occhi mi piove
del lume suo e de la sua vertute;
    le mie bellezze sono al mondo nove,
però che di là su mi son venute:
    le quai non posson esser canosciute
se non da canoscenza d'omo in cui
Amor si metta per piacer altrui.'

    Queste parole si leggon nel viso
d'un'angioletta che ci è apparita:
    e io che per veder lei mirai fiso,
ne sono a rischio di perder la vita;
    però ch'io ricevetti tal ferita
da un ch'io vidi dentro a li occhi sui,
ch'i' vo piangendo e non m'acchetai pui.

64

"Young is my beauty, early yet and new,
I who have come that all of you may see
How fair is that far place which was my country.

I was of heaven and shall return again
To shed my light on all who there abide;
The man who looks, and Love not take him then,
Must put all thought of knowing Love aside;
　For beauty's gifts were mine, not one denied,
When Nature, ladies, asked that He make me
Who willed that you should have my company.

Into my eyes the stars in concert pour
With open hand their virtue and their light;
　Such beauties never dwelt with you before
For mine have come with me from heaven's height:
　And what they are none understands aright
But he to whose heart beauty finds the key
And lets Love in to dwell at liberty."

These words are written on the shining face
Of a young angel who came among us here;
　And I who looked too long upon that grace
Am in such peril I feel my death is near:
　I had a wound to stretch me on my bier
From one her eyes had given hostelry,
And now I weep where peace can never be.

65

Perché ti vedi giovinetta e bella,
tanto che svegli ne la mente Amore,
pres'hai orgoglio e durezza nel core.

Orgogliosa se' fatta e per me dura,
po' che d'ancider me, lasso, ti prove:
    credo che 'l facci per esser sicura
se la vertù d'Amore a morte move.
    Ma perché preso più ch'altro mi trove,
non hai respetto alcun del mi' dolore.
Possi tu spermentar lo suo valore!

65

Because you know you're young in beauty yet
And stir the mind to Love you once look toward,
With pride like stone your maiden heart is barred.

You turn a proud and stonelike face to me
Because you feel my death is worth a try:
I think that you have done it just to see
Whether by force of Love a man can die.
But though you find none loves you more than I,
For grief I bear, you show me no regard.
Love take you then, and let his rule be hard!

Chi guarderà già mai sanza paura
ne li occhi d'esta bella pargoletta,
che m'hanno concio sì, che non s'aspetta
per me se non la morte, che m'è dura?

Vedete quanto è forte mia ventura:
ché fu tra l'altre la mia vita eletta
per dare essemplo altrui, ch'uom non si metta
in rischio di mirar la sua figura.

Destinata mi fu questa finita,
da ch'un uom convenia esser disfatto,
perch'altri fosse di pericol tratto;

e però, lasso, fu' io così ratto
in trarre a me 'l contrario de la vita,
come vertù di stella margherita.

66

And who will ever look without great fear
Into her face whose beauty's young and new
Yet shook me so, I think that nothing's due
To me but death, which comes so cruelly here?

You see that my misfortune was severe
To have myself selected with a view
That I supply the proof that none of you
Should dare to look her way when she is near.

This girl, this death—such were ordained for me,
Since it is best that one of us should die
And others see the danger and pass by;

Therefore, alas, as quickly through the eye
I drank that power from which all life must flee
As pearls in starlight drink in potency.

Amor, che movi tua vertù da cielo
come 'l sol lo splendore,
che là s'apprende più lo suo valore
dove più nobiltà suo raggio trova;
   e come el fuga oscuritate e gelo,
così, alto segnore,
tu cacci la viltate altrui del core,
né ira contra te fa lunga prova:
   da te conven che ciascun ben si mova
per lo qual si travaglia il mondo tutto;
sanza te è distrutto
quanto avemo in potenzia di ben fare,
come pintura in tenebrosa parte,
che non si può mostrare
né dar diletto di color né d'arte.

   Feremi ne lo cor sempre tua luce,
come raggio in la stella,
poi che l'anima mia fu fatta ancella
de la tua podestà primeramente;
   onde ha vita un disio che mi conduce
con sua dolce favella
in rimirar ciascuna cosa bella
con più diletto quanto è più piacente.
   Per questo mio guardar m'è ne la mente
una giovane entrata, che m'ha preso,
e hagli un foco acceso,
com'acqua per chiarezza fiamma accende;
perché nel suo venir li raggi tuoi,
con li quai mi risplende,
saliron tutti su ne gli occhi suoi.

Love, you whose power comes from heaven's hold,
As splendor from the sun,
For his bright strength enkindles most that one
Where most nobility receives his rays;
   Just as he routs obscurity and cold,
High lord, where your writs run
Our hearts can feel their baseness all undone,
Nor does our gloom for long withstand your blaze;
   From you each good derives and perfect praise
Which tirelessly our world of men pursues;
Without you we would lose
All power we possess for doing good
Like paintings hung where shadows have their will
And which so hidden could
Give no delight of color or of skill.

   My heart is held in your lucidity
Like stars with sunlight stayed
Each moment since I knew my soul a maid
To serve your power in whatever kind;
   And hence desire is born which urges me
With tender words for aid
To rest my sight on all that is well made,
With most delight where beauty's most to find.
   And as I stood at gaze, into my mind
A girl, quite young, who took me prisoner, came
And lighted such a flame
As water trapped inside a lens of glass;
Wherefore when she arrived, your long sunrise
Through which she makes me pass
Reverted all into her shining eyes.

Quanto è ne l'esser suo bella, e gentile
ne gli atti ed amorosa,
tanto lo imaginar, che non si posa,
l'adorna ne la mente ov'io la porto;
    non che da se medesmo sia sottile
a così alta cosa,
ma da la tua vertute ha quel ch'elli osa
oltre al poder che natura ci ha porto.
    È sua beltà del tuo valor conforto,
in quanto giudicar si puote effetto
sovra degno suggetto,
in guisa ched è 'l sol segno di foco;
lo qual a lui non dà né to' virtute,
ma fallo in altro loco
ne l'effetto parer di più salute.

    Dunque, segnor di sì gentil natura
che questa nobiltate
che avven qua giuso e tutt'altra bontate
lieva principio de la tua altezza,
    guarda la vita mia quanto ella è dura,
e prendine pietate,
ché lo tuo ardor per la costei bieltate
mi fa nel core aver troppa gravezza.
    Falle sentire, Amor, per tua dolcezza,
il gran disio ch'i' ho di veder lei;
non soffrir che costei
per giovanezza mi conduca a morte:
ché non s'accorge ancor com'ella piace,
né quant'io l'amo forte,
né che ne li occhi porta la mia pace.

As she is fair in being and in act,
Noble and worth Love's care,
My fancy, which no passing moments spare,
Adorns her in my mind, which is her home;
　Though in itself it would have always lacked
The strength to climb that stair
Your virtue gives it courage that it dare
Beyond that limit nature set its own.
　In her great beauty, your power is best shown
(So far as we can judge it by effect
Upon a fit subject),
As fire can represent the sun on earth,
Leaving its power untouched yet making clear
How much the sun is worth
By yielding warmth and light below their sphere.

　And therefore, Lord, whose noble nature shows
That all nobility
Which dwells with us and all benignity
Descended here from your exalted chair,
　Look at my life, how hard a way it goes,
And show you pity me,
For as her beauty feeds your ardency,
My heart is tried beyond what it can bear.
　I pray, with your sweet self, Love, show her there
With what desire of seeing her I bleed,
Nor suffer her to lead
Me to my death by youth that does not guess
To what degree of beauty it has grown,
Or whence comes my distress,
Or how my peace lives in her eyes alone.

Onor ti sarà grande se m'aiuti,
e a me ricco dono,
tanto quanto conosco ben ch'io sono
là 'v'io non posso difender mia vita:
    ché gli spiriti miei son combattuti
da tal, ch'io non ragiono,
se per tua volontà non han perdono,
che possan guari star sanza finita.
    Ed ancor tua potenzia fia sentita
da questa bella donna, che n'è degna:
ché par che si convegna
di darle d'ogni ben gran compagnia,
com'a colei che fu nel mondo nata
per aver segnoria
sovra la mente d'ogni uom che la guata.

Great honor's yours if you can make me sound
And mine a gift of weight,
For I know well that I have reached that date
Where neither life can save itself, nor I:
    She struck my vital spirits to the ground
And left them in such state,
Unless you choose to pardon them their fate,
That I cannot arise and soon must die.
    I pray your power make itself felt by
That lovely woman, who merits it,
For you can see she's fit
To have all good attend her on her way,
As one engendered only to confer
A hunger to obey
Upon the minds of all that look at her.

Io sento sì d'Amor la gran possanza,
ch'io non posso durare
lungamente a soffrire, ond'io mi doglio:
   però che 'l suo valor si pur avanza,
e 'l mio sento mancare
sì ch'io son meno ognora ch'io non soglio.
   Non dico ch'Amor faccia più ch'io voglio,
ché, se facesse quanto il voler chiede,
quella vertù che natura mi diede
nol sosterria, però ch'ella è finita:
ma questo è quello ond'io prendo cordoglio,
che a la voglia il poder non terrà fede;
e se di buon voler nasce merzede,
io l'addimando per aver più vita
da li occhi che nel lor bello splendore
portan conforto ovunque io sento amore.

   Entrano i raggi di questi occhi belli
ne' miei innamorati,
e portan dolce ovunque io sento amaro;
   e sanno lo cammin, sì come quelli
che già vi son passati,
e sanno il loco dove Amor lasciaro,
   quando per li occhi miei dentro il menaro:
per che merzé, volgendosi, a me fanno,
e di colei cui son procaccian danno
celandosi da me, poi tanto l'amo
che sol per lei servir mi tegno caro.
E' miei pensier, che pur d'amor si fanno,
come a lor segno, al suo servigio vanno:
per che l'adoperar sì forte bramo,
che, s'io 'l credesse far fuggendo lei,
lieve saria; ma so ch'io ne morrei.

68

I find the strength of Love so burdensome
To me, I can endure
It only for a time, and so complain.
  For as his powers still increase their sum,
I feel my own less sure,
So that from hour to hour I'm on the wane;
  I'll not say Love exceeds what I'd attain,
For if he did as much as will would try,
That strength which nature sent me from the sky
Could not bear up, faced with infinity,
And this is why my heart's in bitter pain,
That will and strength cannot see eye to eye;
And if good will is what reward's earned by,
I ask it now, that more life come to me
From eyes that in their radiance tell me of
Great comfort every time that I feel love.

  Into my eyes, where Love has come to stay,
Such rays from those eyes pour,
Sour thoughts have flown, and sweetness rules alone;
  These glances know the road, for it was they
Who followed it before
And found the place where Love made me his own
  When through my eyes they led him to his throne:
Turned toward me, then, they bring the joy I've lacked,
But bring her loss by whom I'm bound and racked
If they are turned away—my love is such
I value self for serving her alone.
And all my thoughts, which are of love compact,
As in their cause, serve her in every act;
Wherefore I long for proof of this so much
That if I thought I'd give her it by flight,
I'd leave today—but then I'd die tonight.

Ben è verace amor quel che m'ha preso,
e ben mi stringe forte,
quand'io farei quel ch'io dico per lui:
    ché nullo amore è di cotanto peso,
quanto è quel che la morte
face piacer, per ben servire altrui.
    E io 'n cotal voler fermato fui
sì tosto come il gran disio ch'io sento
fu nato per vertù del piacimento
che nel bel viso d'ogni bel s'accoglie.
Io son servente, e quando penso a cui,
qual ch'ella sia, di tutto son contento:
ché l'uom può ben servir contra talento;
e se merzé giovanezza mi toglie,
io spero tempo che più ragion prenda,
pur che la vita tanto si defenda.

    Quand'io penso un gentil disio, ch'è nato
del gran disio ch'io porto,
ch'a ben far tira tutto il mio podere,
    parmi esser di merzede oltrapagato;
e anche più, ch'a torto
mi par di servidor nome tenere:
    così dinanzi a li occhi del piacere
si fa 'l servir merzé d'altrui bontate.
Ma poi ch'io mi ristringo a veritate,
convien che tal disio servigio conti:
però che, s'io procaccio di valere,
non penso tanto a mia proprïetate
quanto a colei che m'ha in sua podestate,
ché 'l fo perché sua cosa in pregio monti;
e io son tutto suo: così mi tegno,
ch'Amor di tanto onor m'ha fatto degno.

True love it is that holds me close and strait,
And how his grip must hurt
If I'll perform the deeds I promise him!
For there's no love to which we give such weight
As love that can assert
Death for another's sake is glad, not grim.
And this intent possessed my every limb
As soon as the desire I feel this hour
Was born by virtue of great beauty's power,
Which in fair face compounds with all that's fair.
I live in service—joy fills me to the brim
When I consider whose, come sun, come shower,
For men will serve though lady's faces lower.
And if her youth will not reward my care,
I hope for time for her to change her ways,
If life can last until those better days.

When I consider how a fine desire
Born of the desire of years
Has turned to good all strength I had and more,
It seems I've taken too much for my hire,
And worse than wrong appears
That I should bear the name of servitor:
Beneath those eyes where beauty holds the door
And at her side largesse, to serve is pay.
But since I'd keep to truth in what I say,
I'll grant that such desire be titled service:
And though I seek a worth I lacked before,
I take less thought of what may come my way
Than of that one whom all my thoughts obey—
That what she owns may flourish is my purpose,
And she owns all of me; I can be frank,
For Love has made me fit to claim this rank.

Altri ch'Amor non mi potea far tale
ch'eo fosse degnamente
cosa di quella che non s'innamora,
    ma stassi come donna a cui non cale
de l'amorosa mente
che sanza lei non può passare un'ora.
    Io non la vidi tante volte ancora
ch'io non trovasse in lei nova bellezza;
onde Amor cresce in me la sua grandezza
tanto quanto il piacer novo s'aggiugne.
Ond'elli avven che tanto fo dimora
in uno stato, e tanto Amor m'avvezza
con un martiro e con una dolcezza,
quanto è quel tempo che spesso mi pugne,
che dura da ch'io perdo la sua vista
in fino al tempo ch'ella si racquista.

    Canzon mia bella, se tu mi somigli,
tu non sarai sdegnosa
tanto quanto a la tua bontà s'avvene:
    però ti prego che tu t'assottigli,
dolce mia amorosa,
in prender modo e via che ti stea bene.
    Se cavalier t'invita o ti ritene,
imprima che nel suo piacer ti metta,
espia, se far lo puoi, de la sua settta,
se vuoi saver qual è la sua persona:
ché 'l buon col buon sempre camera tene.
Ma elli avven che spesso altri si getta
in compagnia che non è che disdetta
di mala fama ch'altri di lui suona:
con rei non star né a cerchio né ad arte,
ché non fu mai saver tener lor parte.

None else but Love could ever have devised
That I be worthy of
Her ownership who will not pay Love's debt
   But stays a woman who has never prized
The mind that gave her love
And dies the moment that her eyes have set.
   I have not looked at her so often yet
I do not find new beauties in her sight,
Whence Love in me keeps adding to his might
As new delights are added to the last.
Hence comes it that unchanging in his net
I often lie (for Love has bound me tight,
Pain on my left and sweetness on my right)
Until the hours of torment all have passed,
Which start the moment that her face is gone
And end the moment that she brings new dawn.

   My song of love, if you resemble me,
You'll see that pride's to shun,
Though in your case it might be understood.
   I pray you also, walk most carefully,
My sweet, loveworthy one,
In choosing way and manner as you should.
   Should knight make you his guest, or say he would,
Before you put yourself at his command,
Examine, if you're able, all his band,
If you would know what sort he really is:
For good has always shared a room with good
(Though don't forget a hypocrite can stand
Among the good and hide the shameful brand
Of vice in others' excellence, not his).
Avoid the guilty, both his haunts and trade,
For there's a part that wisdom never played.

Canzone, a' tre men rei di nostra terra
te n'anderai prima che vadi altrove:
li due saluta, e 'l terzo vo' che prove
di trarlo fuor di mala setta in pria.
Digli che 'l buon col buon non prende guerra,
prima che co' malvagi vincer prove;
digli ch'è folle chi non si rimove
per tema di vergogna da follia;
ché que' la teme c'ha del mal paura,
per che, fuggendo l'un, l'altro assicura.

My song, seek the three men at home who could
Be blamed the least before you go elsewhere.
Greet the first two, and beg the third one there
That he escape from evil company.
Tell him a good man won't offend the good
Till he has seen how war on bad men fares;
Tell him that it's a fool who never dares
(Lest men should cry, "For shame!") to turn and flee.
He who fears wrong most truly shrinks from shame,
And fleeing one, can scorn the other's name.

Le dolci rime d'amor ch'i solia
cercar ne' miei pensieri
convien ch'io lasci; non perch'io non speri
ad esse ritornare,
    ma perché li atti disdegnosi e feri,
che ne la donna mia
sono appariti, m'han chiusa la via
de l'usato parlare.
    E poi che tempo mi par d'aspettare,
diporrò giù lo mio soave stile,
ch'i' ho tenuto nel trattar d'amore;
e dirò del valore,
per lo qual veramente omo è gentile,
con rima aspr'e sottile;
riprovando 'l giudicio falso e vile
di quei che voglion che di gentilezza
sia principio ricchezza.
E, cominciando, chiamo quel signore
ch'a la mia donna ne li occhi dimora,
per ch'ella di se stessa s'innamora.

    Tale imperò che gentilezza volse,
secondo 'l suo parere,
che fosse antica possession d'avere
con reggimenti belli;
    e altri fu di più lieve savere,
che tal detto rivolse,
e l'ultima particula ne tolse,
ché non l'avea fors'elli!

69

Those words of love which only yesterday
I hunted for my quill,
Farewell; not that I'm not in good hope still
Of writing them once more,
  But haughty looks and gestures of ill-will,
Which now hold utter sway
In my dear lady, have shut and barred the way
To speech I used before.
  And as I have to wait outside the door,
I'll lay aside that delicate style of mine
Which I maintained while love was theme for me
And speak of quality
Which truly noble men bear as their sign
In harsh yet subtle rhyme,
Confuting wholly those who would define
(False view and base) nobility as naught
But what great wealth has bought.
And first I call upon my sovereign, he
Who makes my lady's eyes his throne
That she may fall in love with what's her own.

  There was an emperor ruled upon this cause—
Nobility (he said)
Is gold we've held until its taint has fled
And also charm and grace;
  Then came another of still emptier head
To whom these words gave pause;
He thought he'd cut away that second clause
As doubtless his own case!

Di retro da costui van tutti quelli
che fan gentile per ischiatta altrui
che lungiamente in gran ricchezza è stata;
ed è tanto durata
la così falsa oppinion tra nui,
che l'uom chiama colui
omo gentil che può dicere: 'Io fui
nepote, o figlio, di cotal valente',
benché sia da nïente.
Ma vilissimo sembra, a chi 'l ver guata,
cui è scorto 'l cammino e poscia l'erra,
e tocca a tal, ch'è morto e va per terra!

Chi diffinisce: 'Omo è legno animato',
prima dice non vero,
e, dopo 'l falso, parla non intero;
ma più forse non vede.
Similemente fu chi tenne impero
in diffinire errato,
ché prima puose 'l falso e, d'altro lato,
con difetto procede:
ché le divizie, sì come si crede,
non posson gentilezza dar né tòrre,
però che vili son da lor natura:
poi chi pinge figura,
se non può esser lei, non la può porre,
né la diritta torre
fa piegar rivo che da lungi corre.
Che siano vili appare ed imperfette,
ché, quantunque collette,
non posson quïetar, ma dan più cura;
onde l'animo ch'è dritto e verace
per lor discorrimento non si sface.

Right in their footsteps follows all that race
Which gives the name of "noble" to a man
Who's born where ancient wealth has brought long ease,
And such absurdities
Have been believed in for so long a span
That we accept the sham
And call him nobleman who says, "I am
Grandson of such a worthy, or his son,"
Though his own worth be none.
But worst of all, for him who truly sees,
Is he who knows the road and goes astray
So far, he's dead yet walks the earth today!

Those who would posit, "Man's a conscious tree,"
Say first what is not true
And then stop short before they're really through:
That's all they see perhaps.
Just so that man whom kings were vassals to
Averred what cannot be,
For first he speaks untruth and then, you'll see,
Commits a further lapse:
For wealth (though it's that way most set their caps)
Can neither end nobility nor lend,
As it is in its very nature base;
Thus who would paint a face
Unless he *is* it, will not gain his end,
Nor does a tower bend
If stream refracts and makes its walls distend.
That wealth is base and wants for much, we know,
For let it overflow,
It brings no peace but aggravates your case;
Wherefore the mind whose way is true and straight
Should not be grieved if he escape its weight.

Né voglion che vil uom gentil divegna,
né di vil padre scenda
nazion che per gentil già mai s'intenda;
questo è da lor confesso:
    onde lor ragion par che sé offenda
in tanto quanto assegna
che tempo a gentilezza si convegna,
diffinendo con esso.
    Ancor, segue di ciò che innanzi ho messo,
che siam tutti gentili o ver villani,
o che non fosse ad uom cominciamento:
ma ciò io non consento,
ned ellino altressì, se son cristiani!
Per che a 'ntelletti sani
è manifesto i lor diri esser vani,
e io così per falsi li riprovo,
e da lor mi rimovo;
e dicer voglio omai, sì com'io sento,
che cosa è gentilezza, e da che vene,
e dirò i segni che 'l gentile uom tene.

    Dico ch'ogni vertù principalmente
vien da una radice:
vertute, dico, che fa l'uom felice
in sua operazione.
    Questo è, secondo che l'Etica dice,
un abito eligente
lo qual dimora in mezzo solamente,
e tai parole pone.
    Dico che nobiltate in sua ragione
importa sempre ben del suo subietto,
come viltate importa sempre male;
e vertute cotale
dà sempre altrui di sé buono intelletto;

No man that's base can found a noble line,
No man of base descent
Can be ennobled—that's their argument,
And they need say no more.
    Here you can see that if they've really meant
To say one must define
Nobility as somehow linked to time,
Logic flies out the door.
    It follows then from what I've said before
That we are gentles or plebeians all
Or Eve knew someone else while Adam slept;
And this I'll not accept,
Nor they besides, if they seek heaven's hall!
Who's saner than King Saul
Can tell their reasonings break upon this wall,
And thus I show they err in root and stem
And stand apart from them;
And now I'll say (which I have overleapt)
What thing's nobility, whence it derives,
And by what signs we reckon noble lives.

    Each virtue shares a common origin
And on its bidding waits:
Virtue, I mean, which when it operates
Brings men to happiness.
    That is, as Aristotle's Ethics states,
A habit resting in
Choice of the mean in every tide and wind—
No more is said, no less.
    Nobility that's such as I'd express
Implies a good in him who bears its name,
As baseness, evil, though wealth would make us blind;
And virtue as defined
Is always good no matter whence it came;

131

per che in medesmo detto
convegnono ambedue, ch'en d'uno effetto.
Onde convien da l'altra vegna l'una,
o d'un terzo ciascuna;
ma se l'una val ciò che l'altra vale,
e ancor più, da lei verrà più tosto.
E ciò ch'io dett'ho qui sia per supposto.

È gentilezza dovunqu'è vertute,
ma non vertute ov'ella;
sì com'è 'l cielo dovunqu'è la stella,
ma ciò non *e converso*.
E noi in donna e in età novella
vedem questa salute,
in quanto vergognose son tenute,
ch'è da vertù diverso.
Dunque verrà, come dal nero il perso,
ciascheduna vertute da costei,
o vero il gener lor, ch'io misi avanti.
Però nessun si vanti
dicendo: 'Per ischiatto io son con lei',
ch'elli son quasi dei
quei c'han tal grazia fuor di tutti rei:
ché solo Iddio a l'anima la dona
che vede in sua persona
perfettamente star: sì ch'ad alquanti
che seme di felicità sia costa,
messo da Dio ne l'anima ben posta.

L'anima cui adorna esta bontate
non la si tiene ascosa,
ché dal principio ch'al corpo si sposa
la mostra infin la morte.

Defining thus we frame
Words fitting both, for their effect's the same.
Hence this derives from that—we've all concurred—
Or both from still a third;
If one includes all that its mate's assigned
And more besides, it has to be the source—
In all below let this remain in force.

  Nobility is found in virtue's sphere
But she holds more by far,
Just as there's sky wherever there's a star
But not conversely so.
  We see in women and in those who are
Still young this good appear
So far as shamefastness has kept them clear,
Which is not virtue though.
  Then every virtue, as black is source to sloe,
Derives its being from nobility
Or what they share, as I have said above.
Let none go boasting of
His birth and say, "My noble family tree . . . ,"
For they would seem to be
Like gods who in this grace live flawlessly,
For God alone will grant it to that soul
Whose body makes a whole,
Each wed to each; and so to those who love
Wisdom, nobility's a seed of joy
Which God has closed in soul of good alloy.

  The soul who takes this goodness as her gauge
Won't hide it from the light
But from the moment soul and flesh unite
Displays it till her last.

Ubidente, soave e vergognosa
è ne la prima etate,
e sua persona adorna di bieltate
con le sue parti accorte;
    in giovinezza, temperata e forte,
piena d'amore e di cortese lode,
e solo in lealtà far si diletta;
è ne la sua senetta
prudente e giusta, a larghezza se n'ode,
e 'n se medesma gode
d'udire e ragionar de l'altrui prode;
poi ne la quarta parte de la vita
a Dio si rimarita,
contemplando la fine che l'aspetta,
e benedice li tempi passati.
Vedete omai quanti son l'ingannati!

    Contra-li-erranti mia, tu te n'andrai;
e quando tu sarai
in parte dove sia la donna nostra,
non le tenere il tuo mestier coverto:
tu le puoi dir per certo:
'Io vo parlando de l'amica vostra.'

Obedient, tender, shy of human sight
Is she in her first age
And beauty walks beside her as her page
With all that suits her best;
    Her prime is poised and valiant at the test,
Fulfilled in love and courteous in all ways,
And takes delight in what Law bids her do.
Then fading years ensue,
Prudent and just; her open hand wins praise,
She joys in every phrase
She speaks and hears which others' virtues raise.
Then when old age is standing at her side
Again she's God's own bride
Intent upon the end she hastens to
And thinking benediction on old times.
How many wanderers need to hear these rhymes!

My "Scourge-for-strays," it's time that you were gone,
And when you've journeyed on
To where our lady looks at what I send,
Do not conceal why you're a visitor
But boldly say to her,
"My conversation's wholly of your friend."

Poscia ch'Amor del tutto m'ha lasciato,
non per mio grato,
ché stato non avea tanto gioioso,
ma però che pietoso
fu tanto del meo core,
che non sofferse d'ascoltar suo pianto;
  i' canterò così disamorato
contra 'l peccato,
ch'è nato in noi, di chiamare a ritroso
tal ch'è vile e noioso
con nome di valore,
cioè di leggiadria, ch'è bella tanto
  che fa degno di manto
imperïal colui dov'ella regna:
ell'è verace insegna
la qual dimostra u' la vertù dimora;
per ch'io son certo, se ben la difendo
nel dir com'io la 'ntendo,
ch'Amor di sé mi farà grazia ancora.

  Sono che per gittar via loro avere
credon potere
capere là dove li boni stanno,
che dopo morte fanno
riparo ne la mente
a quei cotanti c'hanno canoscenza.
  Ma lor messione a' bon non pò piacere;
per che tenere
savere fora, e fuggiriano il danno,
che si aggiugne a lo 'nganno
di loro e de la gente
c'hanno falso iudicio in lor sentenza.

136

70

Now that lord Love has quite abandoned me,
Not at my plea
Whom he gave joy I never knew before,
But all because he bore
Such pity of my heart
He could no longer stay and hear it weep,
  I'll sing, since I am free,
Against a sin that we
Can see is ours, to claim against all lore
Who's vile, disgusting, more,
Has played a worthy part,
That is, of gallantry, whose beauty's deep
  Enough he ought to sleep
In royal robes in whom this grace prevails;
Its banner never fails
To mark the house where virtue long has been,
And I am sure, if I can well defend
The meaning I intend,
That Love will take me to his grace again.

  There're men who throwing all their wealth away
Hope we will say
Their way lies on the road that good men tread
Which leads when we are dead
To memory in the mind
Of those whose good opinion all men prize.
  But none of sense approves of such display—
Better if they
Would stay their hand and keep their wealth instead,
Not add to foolishness which has misled
These wastrels and that kind
Which worships them and thinks that it is wise.

Qual non dirà fallenza
divorar cibo ed a lussuria intendere?
ornarsi, come vendere
si dovesse al mercato di non saggi?
ché 'l saggio non pregia om per vestimenta,
ch'altrui sono ornamenta,
ma pregia il senno e li genti coraggi.

E altri son che, per esser ridenti,
d'intendimenti
correnti voglion esser iudicati
da quei che so' ingannati
veggendo rider cosa
che lo 'ntelletto cieco non la vede.
E' parlan con vocaboli eccellenti;
vanno spiacenti,
contenti che da lunga sian mirati;
non sono innamorati
mai di donna amorosa;
ne' parlamenti lor tengono scede;
non moveriano il piede
per donneare a guisa di leggiadro,
ma come al furto il ladro,
così vanno a pigliar villan diletto;
e non però che 'n donne è sì dispento
leggiadro portamento,
che paiono animai sanza intelletto.

Ancor che ciel con cielo in punto sia,
che leggiadria
disvia cotanto, e più che quant'io conto,
io, che le sono conto
merzé d'una gentile
che la mostrava in tutti gli atti sui,

Who is it that denies
Pursuit of feasts and bedplay's a deceit?
Tricked out, as if to meet
Your buyer in a marketplace of fools?
The wise give none esteem for what he wears
And all can buy at fairs
But for high heart, and head which good sense rules.

And there's the sort who laughs and never quits
And hopes that it's
"Quick-wits" will be the compliment he's paid
By those who are afraid
To show the cause for mirth
Has passed too fast for their slow wits to seize.
He likes impressive language, not what fits,
Preens at his own good bits,
And sits content with distant accolade.
Love never touched this blade
For ladies of true worth;
His usual talk is all in flippancies,
    Nor will he forfeit ease
To pay that court no gallant man would shirk,
But like a thief at work
Goes forth to steal a vile and brief delight
Without excuse—our ladies do not flee
The way of courtesy
To live like beasts who lack all human light.

    Since heaven commands, and stars have made it clear,
The way that we're
To steer has strayed, farther than words can go,
I, who have come to know
It thanks to a noble one
Who took it as her path and never fell,

non tacerò di lei, ché villania
far mi parria
sì ria, ch'a' suoi nemici sarei giunto:
per che da questo punto
con rima più sottile
tratterò il ver di lei, ma non so cui.
    Eo giuro per colui
ch'Amor si chiama ed è pien di salute,
che sanza ovrar vertute
nessun pote acquistar verace loda:
dunque, se questa mia matera è bona,
come ciascun ragiona,
sarà vertù o con vertù s'annoda.

    Non è pura vertù la disvïata,
poi ch'è blasmata,
negata là 'v'è più vertù richesta,
cioè in gente onesta
di vita spiritale
o in abito che di scïenza tiene.
    Dunque, s'ell'è in cavalier lodata,
sarà mischiata,
causata di più cose; per che questa
conven che di sé vesta
l'un bene e l'altro male,
ma vertù pura in ciascuno sta bene.
    Sollazzo è che convene
con esso Amore e l'opera perfetta:
da questo terzo retta
è vera leggiadria e in esser dura,
sì come il sole al cui esser s'adduce
lo calore e la luce
con la perfetta sua bella figura.

I'll always write of it lest silence here
Make me appear
To fear so basely I would be its foe;
And from this time I'll show
In verse more finely done
The truth of it—for whom, I cannot tell.
  I swear by him as well
Whose name is Love, whose goodness is unique—
Where virtues are to seek
No one will find true praise accorded him.
Wherefore, if all agree my theme is good
(And there is none but would),
Virtue it is or virtue's next of kin.

  This errant grace is virtue, yet not all,
Since from that hall
Some wall it out where virtue must be had,
That is, where men are glad
To mortify their will
Or give perfected knowledge all their care.
  And though to every knight who heeds its call
High praises fall,
Withal its birth is mixed; both good and bad,
This way has always clad
One well, another ill,
But unmixed virtue anyone can wear.
  There is a Joy to square
With Love and perfect Innocence of deeds:
In such a tripling breeds
True gallantry, sprung of a hardy race,
Just like the sun, for whose existence meet
Great brilliance and great heat
And beauty which is perfect in his face.

Al gran pianeto è tutta simigliante
che, dal levante
avante infino a tanto che s'asconde,
co li bei raggi infonde
vita e vertù qua giuso
ne la matera sì com'è è disposta:
   e questa, disdegnosa di cotante
persone, quante
sembiante portan d'omo, e non responde
il lor frutto a le fronde
per lo mal c'hanno in uso,
simili beni al cor gentile accosta;
   ché 'n donar vita è tosta
co' bei sembianti e co' begli atti novi
ch'ognora par che trovi,
e vertù per essemplo a chi lei piglia.
Oh falsi cavalier, malvagi e rei,
nemici di costei,
ch'al prenze de le stelle s'assimiglia!

   Dona e riceve l'om cui questa vole,
mai non sen dole;
né 'l sole per donar luce a le stelle,
né per prender da elle
nel suo effetto aiuto;
ma l'uno e l'altro in ciò diletto tragge.
   Già non s'induce a ira per parole,
ma quelle sole
ricole che son bone, e sue novelle
sono leggiadre e belle;
per sé caro è tenuto
e disïato da persone sagge,

With the bright sun in every way this vies
Which in the skies
From rise until his yellow beams are shorn
Instills with light like corn
Vigor and life on earth,
As great a share to each as each can lift.
  For gallantry, who turns disdainful eyes
On each who tries
Disguise as man and yet has never borne
Fruit that his leaves have sworn
(Evil undoes its birth),
To noble hearts accords the self-same gift:
  His boons of life are swift
With charming looks and gracious deeds that you
Would think were ever new,
And swift the virtue lent his avatars.
O would-be knights, untrue and full of sin,
Who lay your traps for him
That takes his model from the prince of stars!

  He gives and takes, who makes this grace his aim,
As if in game;
The same the sun, in giving stars his beams
Or calling on their gleams
For help at east and west:
This way for each the greatest pleasure lies.
  He does not flare in anger at a name
But will acclaim
What came with good intent, and his own themes
Are gallant as beseems;
And thus he's in request
And held most dear by people that are wise;

ché de l'altre selvagge
cotanto laude quanto biasmo prezza;
per nessuna grandezza
monta in orgoglio, ma quando gl'incontra
che sua franchezza li conven mostrare,
quivi si fa laudare.
Color che vivon fanno tutti contra.

As for barbarians' cries,
He rates their blame no higher than their praise
And lets no grandeur raise
His heart to pride, but when the time is fit
For him to show his spirit or to fall,
He leaves with praise from all.
Those living now do just the opposite.

Due donne in cima de la mente mia
venute sono a ragionar d'amore:
l'una ha in sé cortesia e valore,
prudenza e onestà in compagnia;

l'altra ha bellezza e vaga leggiadria,
adorna gentilezza le fa onore:
e io, merzé del dolce mio signore,
mi sto a piè de la lor signoria.

Parlan Bellezza e Virtù a l'intelletto,
e fan quistion come un cor puote stare
intra due donne con amor perfetto.

Risponde il fonte del gentil parlare
ch'amar si può bellezza per diletto,
e puossi amar virtù per operare.

71

Talking of Love and failing to agree,
Two women scale the summit of my mind:
With one come Worth and Courtesy behind,
Prudence, Uprightness too, in company;

The other brings Good Looks and Gaiety,
And for her maid-of-honor, Noble Kind—
While I (thanks to my Lord, who's author) find
I'm at the feet of their authority.

Beauty and Virtue call my intellect
To settle how a heart can stand between
Two ladies and still love without defect:

The spring of noble speaking told each queen
That virtue earns our love by its effect
And beauty by delight when it is seen.

72

Chi udisse tossir la malfatata
moglie di Bicci vocato Forese,
potrebbe dir ch'ell'ha forse vernata
ove si fa 'l cristallo, in quel paese.

Di mezzo agosto la truove infreddata:
or sappi che de' far d'ogni altro mese!
e non le val perché dorma calzata,
merzé del copertoio c'ha cortonese. . . .

La tosse, 'l freddo e l'altra mala voglia
non l'addovien per omor ch'abbia vecchi,
ma per difetto ch'ella sente al nido.

Piange la madre, c'ha più d'una doglia,
dicendo: 'Lassa, che per fichi secchi
messa l'avre' 'n casa del conte Guido!'

Whoever heard her coughing, the poor dear,
That wife of Bicci's (keep your windows shut!),
Would say she must have wintered north of here
Where wind makes crystal, in some Lappish hut.

Mid-August leaves her cold as corpse on bier;
The other months, she'd be—imagine what. . . .
No use her sleeping dressed in all her gear:
She has a covering that's inadequate.

Her cough, her cold, her other maladies
Were not incurred because she's getting grey
But from a lack she suffers in her nest.

Her mother weeps, whose woes would fill the seas,
Saying, "Alas, for two dry figs, I'd lay,
She could have had Count Guido and his crest."

72a   (FORESE DONATI)

L'altra notte mi venne una gran tosse,
perch'i' non avea che tener a dosso;
ma incontanente che fu dì, fui mosso
per gir a guadagnar ove che fosse.

Udite la fortuna ove m'addosse:
ch'i' credetti trovar perle in un bosso
e be' fiorin coniati d'oro rosso;
ed i' trovai Alaghier tra le fosse,

legato a nodo ch'i' non saccio 'l nome,
se fu di Salamone o d'altro saggio.
Allora mi segna' verso 'l levante:

e que' mi disse: 'Per amor di Dante,
scio'mi.' Ed i' non potti veder come:
tornai a dietro, e compie' mi' vïaggio.

72a

All night last night I coughed and coughed—you see,
I'd nothing near to keep my back from cold,
But soon as it was light, I roused and strolled
Off to seek gain wherever it might be.

Listen, and hear the luck that guided me.
I thought I'd find a box with pearls to hold
And florins finely minted of red gold
But found your father, in the graveyard—he

Was in a knot I couldn't name you now,
The work of Solomon or some other mage.
I crossed myself, my face turned toward daybreak,

And heard him groan at me, "For Dante's sake,
Untie me." Since I couldn't figure how,
I went back home, and there I write this page.

Ben ti faranno il nodo Salamone,
Bicci novello, e' petti de le starne,
ma peggio fia la lonza del castrone,
ché 'l cuoio farà vendetta de la carne;

tal che starai più presso a San Simone,
se tu non ti procacci de l'andarne:
e 'ntendi che 'l fuggire el mal boccone
sarebbe oramai tardi a ricomprarne.

Ma ben m'è detto che tu sai un'arte
che, s'egli è vero, tu ti puoi rifare,
però ch'ell'è di molto gran guadagno;

e fa sì, a tempo, che tema di carte
non hai, che ti bisogni scioperare;
ma ben ne colse male a' fi' di Stagno.

73

Bicci my boy, the partridges you eat
Will snare you worse than knots of Solomon;
And racks of lamb, oh my!—for all that meat
Sheepskins prepare a reckoning, one by one.

That prison on the corner of the street
Will move you closer soon, unless you run;
And mind you, don't expect to beat the heat
By dieting—the damage has been done.

But how could I forget! You have a trade
By which you can recoup, or so I've heard—
Small fortunes are just lying round here loose.

And for a while you needn't be afraid
The skins will clip your wings. Eat undeterred!
What if thieves end up paying through the noose?

73a (FORESE DONATI)

Va' rivesti San Gal prima che dichi
parole o motti d'altrui povertate,
ché troppo n'è venuta gran pietate
in questo verno a tutti suoi amichi.

E anco, se tu ci hai per sì mendichi,
perché pur mandi a noi per caritate?
Dal castello Altrafonte ha' ta' grembiate
ch'io saccio ben che tu te ne nutrichi.

Ma ben ti lecerà il lavorare,
se Dio ti salvi la Tana e 'l Francesco,
che col Belluzzo tu non stia in brigata.

A lo spedale a Pinti ha' riparare;
e già mi par vedere stare a desco,
ed in terzo, Alighier co la farsata.

73a

Go reimburse San Gal before you cast
Aspersions on another's poverty,
For your demands meant grievous misery
To all its "friends" this bitter winter past.

And if you think bare purses make us fast,
Why do you send to us for charity?
The Altrafronte House, we all can see,
Has clothed your back and filled your bowl with mast.

You're amply paid, and should be quite content,
If God spares kinsmen Tana and Francesco
So you don't join your uncle on the street!

At last to Pinti spital you'll be sent—
I see already how you'll stand al fresco,
Ragged, with beggars, waiting for a seat.

Bicci novel, figliuol di non so cui,
s'i' non ne domandasse monna Tessa,
giù per la gola tanta roba hai messa,
ch'a forza ti convien torre l'altrui.

E già la gente si guarda da lui,
chi ha borsa a lato, là dov'e' s'appressa,
dicendo: 'Questi c'ha la faccia fessa
è piùvico ladron negli atti sui.'

E tal giace per lui nel letto tristo,
per tema non sia preso a lo 'mbolare,
che gli appartien quanto Giosepp' a Cristo.

Di Bicci e de' fratei posso contare
che, per lo sangue lor, del male acquisto
sanno a lor donne buon cognati stare.

74

Bicci my boy, you son of God-knows-who
(Though I could ask your mother—if she knows),
Your goods diminish as your belly grows
And stealing now must keep it full for you.

Already people when he passes through
Look grimly, hands on purses, where he goes,
And say, "That fellow with the broken nose
Is Public Thief—he needs a rope or two."

And "father" lies at home all night half-dead
With fear lest one be taken at his "job"
Who owes him what Christ owed Joseph's work abed.

Bicci and his two brothers—all that mob
Like sisters treat the women that they've wed
And pay a husband's dues with what they rob.

74a   (FORESE DONATI)

Ben so che fosti figliuol d'Alaghieri,
ed accorgomen pur a la vendetta
che facesti di lui sì bella e netta
de l'aguglin ched e' cambiò l'altr'ieri.

Se tagliato n'avessi uno a quartieri,
di pace non dovevi aver tal fretta;
ma tu ha' poi sì piena la bonetta,
che non la porterebber duo somieri.

Buon uso ci ha' recato, ben til dico,
che qual ti carica ben di bastone,
colui ha' per fratello e per amico.

Il nome ti direi de le persone
che v'hanno posto su; ma del panico
mi reca, ch'i' vo' metter la ragione.

74a

Oh, you were Alighieri's son, I'd say—
No doubt of it—no question—we can tell
By that exemplary revenge which fell
On them who clipped his coins "the other day."

Though you had quartered one to make him pay,
No need for talk of peace to come pell-mell;
But fear has filled your trousers up so well
Two pack-mules couldn't carry them away.

A noble usage this, it seems to us,
To treat those men who thrash you till they're hot
As friends and kin, and so avoid a fuss.

I'll give their names, the ones that you've "forgot"
Who banked on you—but first, my abacus
Needs one more string, if I'm to count the lot.

75a

Dante Alleghier, d'ogni senno pregiato
che in corpo d'om si potesse trovare,
un tuo amico di debile affare
da la tua parte s'era richiamato

a una donna, che l'ha sì incolpato
con fini spade di sottil tagliare,
che in nulla guisa ne pensa scampare,
però che' colpi han già il cor toccato.

Onde a te cade farne alta vendetta
di quella che l'ha sì forte conquiso
che null'altra mai non se ne inframetta.

Delle sue condizioni io vi diviso,
ch'ell'è una leggiadra giovinetta
che porta propiamente Amor nel viso.

75a

Dante Alighieri, who walk in widest fame
For all the wisdom mind of man can bear,
One of your friends, whose life's no great affair,
Has made an accusation in your name

Against a lady who said he was to blame
Though she had struck with such an edge of care
That of his life he thinks he must despair—
Meant for his heart, her blows have reached their aim.

To you it falls to take revenge for me
On her whose blows have left me in such case
No woman else will think I'm fit to see.

This do I tell you of her worth and grace,
That she has youth and charm and gaiety
And carries Love himself within her face.

75

Io Dante a te che m'hai così chiamato
rispondo brieve con poco pensare,
però che più non posso soprastare,
tanto m'ha 'l tuo pensier forte affannato.

Ma ben vorrei saper dove e in qual lato
ti richiamasti, per me ricordare:
forse che per mia lettera mandare
saresti d'ogni colpo risanato.

Ma s'ella è donna che porti anco vetta,
sì 'n ogni parte mi pare esser fiso
ch'ella verrà a farti gran disdetta.

Secondo detto m'hai ora, m'avviso
che ella è sì d'ogni peccato netta
come angelo che stia in paradiso.

75

Dante to you, who called upon his name,
Returns few words and plucks them from the air—
Not one short moment more could he forbear,
Your words brought so much sorrow when they came.

It's best that you should tell him, all the same,
Whom you accused in his name, when, and where;
Perhaps a letter he could send her there
Would heal you of the injuries you claim.

But if her wedding-day is still to be,
I'm sure that at another time and place
She will retract what made you disagree.

I'd judge by what you've written of this case
That she is clear of fault as utterly
As is an angel there before God's face.

Messer Brunetto, questa pulzelletta
con esso voi si ven la pasqua a fare:
non intendete pasqua di mangiare,
ch'ella non mangia, anzi vuol esser letta.

La sua sentenzia non richiede fretta,
né luogo di romor né da giullare;
anzi si vuol più volte lusingare
prima che 'n intelletto altrui si metta.

Se voi non la intendete in questa guisa,
in vostra gente ha molti frati Alberti
da intender ciò ch'è posto loro in mano.

Con lor vi restringete sanza risa;
e se li altri de' dubbi non son certi,
ricorrete a la fine a messer Giano.

Chez vous, Brunetto, this girl will rest her head
All Easter-Feast—see it's the proper sort
And not the feaster's Easter that's your forte:
She does not eat, she wishes to be read.

Her meaning's lost on those who gulp their bread
Or haunt jongleurs and other noisy sport;
In fact, you'll often have to pay her court
Before you're really clear on what she's said.

And if you're baffled by her subtleties,
Your circle will provide you those wise owls
Who grasp what men have put into their hand.

Go join them now, but stop the giggling, please;
And if the hard parts leave them wreathed in scowls,
Perhaps good Master Zany'd understand.

77

Io son venuto al punto de la rota
che l'orizzonte, quando il sol si corca,
ci partorisce il geminato cielo,
    e la stella d'amor ci sta remota
per lo raggio lucente che la 'nforca
sì di traverso, che le si fa velo;
    e quel pianeta che conforta il gelo
si mostra tutto a noi per lo grand'arco
nel qual ciascun di sette fa poca ombra:
e però non disgombra
un sol penser d'amore, ond'io son carco,
la mente mia, ch'è più dura che petra
in tener forte imagine di petra.

    Levasi de la rena d'Etïopia
lo vento peregrin che l'aere turba,
per la spera del sol ch'ora la scalda;
    e passa il mare, onde conduce copia
di nebbia tal, che, s'altro non la sturba,
questo emisperio chiude tutto e salda;
    e poi si solve, e cade in bianca falda
di fredda neve ed in noiosa pioggia,
onde l'aere s'attrista tutto e piagne:
e Amor, che sue ragne
ritira in alto pel vento che poggia,
non m'abbandona; sì è bella donna
questa crudel che m'è data per donna.

    Fuggito è ogne augel che 'l caldo segue
del paese d'Europa, che non perde
le sette stelle gelide unquemai;

Heaven's wheel (my scaffold) has brought me to that place
Where the horizon, when the sun declines,
Delivers up those Twins day kept in hold,
    And the evening star, Love's own, withdraws her grace
Westward behind an arm of light, which shines
So thwarting her, she takes a veil of gold;
    And Saturn, that lord who urges on the cold
Exalts himself under the Crab's long arch
To which the seven planets bring small shade:
Yet I cannot dissuade
One thought from Love, who rides me as I march
In my contracted heart, harder than rock
Though close adherence to a shape of rock.

    Look southward now, where from Egyptian sands
The alien wind at which our sky turns gray
Strides from the sphere of the sun and from heat's height
    Over the sea, driving before him bands
Of cloud such, if no other block his way,
He shuts our half-world in and welds it tight,
    And then dissolves, and falls minutely white
Frozen to snow or loosed to weary rain,
Whence all our sky has saddened into tears;
And Love, when the wind veers
Into his face, pulls up both line and seine,
Yet stays with me, she is so fair a woman,
My cruel mistress, my appointed woman.

    All birds have taken flight now, all that long
For warmth, from Europe which has never seen
Its heaven clear of seven stars of ice,

e li altri han posto a le lor voci triegue
per non sonarle infino al tempo verde,
se ciò non fosse per cagion di guai;
   e tutti li animali che son gai
di lor natura, son d'amor disciolti,
però che 'l freddo lor spirito ammorta:
e 'l mio più d'amor porta;
ché li dolzi pensier non mi son tolti
né mi son dati per volta di tempo,
ma donna li mi dà c'ha picciol tempo.

   Passato hanno lor termine le fronde
che trasse fuor la vertù d'Arïete
per adornare il mondo, e morta è l'erba;
   ramo di foglia verde a noi s'asconde
se non se in lauro, in pino o in abete
o in alcun che sua verdura serba;
   e tanto è la stagion forte ed acerba,
c'ha morti li fioretti per le piagge,
li quai non poten tollerar la brina:
e la crudele spina
però Amor di cor non la mi tragge;
per ch'io son fermo di portarla sempre
ch'io sarò in vita, s'io vivesse sempre.

   Versan le vene le fummifere acque
per li vapor che la terra ha nel ventre,
che d'abisso li tira suso in alto;
   onde cammino al bel giorno mi piacque
che ora è fatto rivo, e sarà mentre
che durerà del verno il grande assalto;
   la terra fa un suol che par di smalto,
e l'acqua morta si converte in vetro
per la freddura che di fuor la serra:

And the rest have set a truce upon their song,
Untuned and mute until the year be green,
Except when grief has lashed them into cries;
  And all those living things whose natures rise
In joy, have slipped the chain and snare of Love
For cold has numbed their spirits to the core
And Love loads mine the more,
For these sweet thoughts I bear will not remove,
Nor are they given, by season or by time:
She gave me them who's hardly entered time.

All out of date, the leaves are brittle veins
Whose sleeping buds the Ram had set astir
That earth might move in beauty, and grass is sere;
  For us no limb of leafy green remains
Unless on pine, on laurel, or on fir,
Or other tree whose leafage lasts all year.
  The time is so unripe we suffer here,
It killed the weak wildflowers at its start
With rime and hoar-frost that could not be borne;
And yet Love's cruel thorn
Has not been taken from my aching heart,
For I am set on wearing it always,
My whole life long, though life were mine always.

In seam and channel spumes of water run
Smoky with vapors earth amassed below
And now returns through cavern, sill, and fault;
  Where paths were pleasant in my days of sun,
Each now is bed for brooks, and will be so
While the lord Winter presses his assault;
  Earth is enameled, ringing like a vault,
And the dead water clenches into glass
Where cold stoops down and takes it in his grip;

e io de la mia guerra
non son però tornato un passo a retro,
né vo' tornar; ché, se 'l martiro è dolce,
la morte de' passare ogni altro dolce.

Canzone, or che sarà di me ne l'altro
dolce tempo novello, quando piove
amore in terra da tutti li cieli,
quando per questi geli
amore è solo in me, e non altrove?
Saranne quello ch'è d'un uom di marmo,
se in pargoletta fia per core un marmo.

And yet not one short step
Have I retreated, though at such a pass,
Nor will retreat, for if this pain be sweet,
Death must excel all else that we think sweet.

My song, what will become of me, what then
In that new season's sweetness when he rains,
Love, the young Love on earth from every heaven
When Love, despite the Seven,
In me alone, and nowhere else, remains?
I shall be such as is a man of marble
If in her heart this tender girl prove marble.

Al poco giorno e al gran cerchio d'ombra
son giunto, lasso, ed al bianchir de' colli,
quando si perde lo color ne l'erba:
e 'l mio disio però non cangia il verde,
sì è barbato ne la dura petra
che parla e sente come fosse donna.

Similemente questa nova donna
si sta gelata come neve a l'ombra;
ché non la move, se non come petra,
il dolce tempo che riscalda i colli,
e che li fa tornar di bianco in verde
perché li copre di fioretti e d'erba.

Quand'ella ha in testa una ghirlanda d'erba,
trae de la mente nostra ogn'altra donna;
perché si mischia il crespo giallo e 'l verde
sì bel, ch'Amor lì viene a stare a l'ombra,
che m'ha serrato intra piccioli colli
più forte assai che la calcina petra.

La sua bellezza ha più vertù che petra,
e l' colpo suo non può sanar per erba;
ch'io son fuggito per piani e per colli,
per potere scampar da cotal donna;
e dal suo lume non mi può far ombra
poggio né muro mai né fronda verde.

Io l'ho veduta già vestita a verde,
sì fatta ch'ella avrebbe messo in petra
l'amor ch'io porto pur a la sua ombra:

78

To dwindling day and the great ring of shadow
Alas, I've climbed, and whitening of the hills
When winter takes all color from the grass—
Yet my desire will never be less green,
So barbed is he into the stubborn rock
Which speaks and feels as if it were a woman.

As stiff she stands herself, this new-found woman
Annealed by frost and thaw, old snow in shadow,
And does not move, or moves as moves rock
To that sweet time which suns the naked hills
And strips their winter whiteness down to green
That they may lie in flowers and in grass.

When to her head she lifts a crown of grass,
Our mind is dark to any other woman,
For there commingle yellow and crisp green
So finely, Love makes their shade his shadow,
Love who has locked me up in two small hills
More tightly than a sea-shell lost in rock.

Strength in her beauty is stronger than in rock
And wounds it gives will find no healing grass:
So I have fled through plains and over hills
And hoped to find the limits of this woman
But her enormous light disdains a shadow
From knoll or wall or sheltering boughs of green.

So have I seen her standing dressed in green,
So artificed, she would have lifted rock
Into that love in which I love her shadow—

ond'io l'ho chesta in un bel prato d'erba,
innamorata com'anco fu donna,
e chiuso intorno d'altissimi colli.

Ma ben ritorneranno i fiumi a' colli,
prima che questo legno molle e verde
s'infiammi, come suol far bella donna,
di me; che mi torrei dormire in petra
tutto il mio tempo e gir pascendo l'erba,
sol per veder do' suoi panni fanno ombra.

Quandunque i colli fanno più nera ombra,
sotto un bel verde la giovane donna
la fa sparer, com'uom petra sott'erba.

Hence I have dreamed her set in meadow-grass,
Heart-deep in love, as deep as ever woman,
And circled with a ring of leaning hills.

But first these streams will turn and climb their hills
Before that standing wood, so lithe and green,
Take flame, such flame as knows so fair a woman,
And that flame mine; meanwhile to couch on rock
In every season, to give my hunger grass,
And eyes cast down, to glimpse her train of shadow.

Wherever hills rise up from darkest shadow,
Behind a sleeve of green this maiden-woman
Obscures their darkness, like a rock in grass.

Amor, tu vedi ben che questa donna
la tua vertù non cura in alcun tempo,
che suol de l'altre belle farsi donna;
e poi s'accorse ch'ell'era mia donna
per lo tuo raggio ch'al volto mi luce,
d'ogne crudelità si fece donna;
 sì che non par ch'ell'abbia cor di donna
ma di qual fiera l'ha d'amor più freddo;
ché per lo tempo caldo e per lo freddo
mi fa sembiante pur come una donna
che fosse fatta d'una bella petra
per man di quei che me' intagliasse in petra.

 E io, che son costante più che petra
in ubidirti per bieltà di donna,
porto nascoso il colpo de la petra,
con la qual tu mi desti come a petra
che t'avesse innoiato lungo tempo,
tal che m'andò al core ov'io son petra.
 E mai non si scoperse alcuna petra
o da splendor di sole o da sua luce,
che tanta avesse né vertù né luce
che mi potesse atar da questa petra,
sì ch'ella non mi meni col suo freddo
colà dov'io sarò di morte freddo.

 Segnor, tu sai che per algente freddo
l'acqua diventa cristallina petra
là sotto tramontana ov'è il gran freddo,
e l'aere sempre in elemento freddo
vi si converte, sì che l'acqua è donna
in quella parte per cagion del freddo:

You, Love, you must see clearly how this woman
Cares nothing for your power at any time
Though it is lord to every other woman;
And when she saw I loved her as a woman
By your bright presence in which my face is light,
All cruelty took possession of this woman;
   And now it seems her heart is not of woman
But of a beast whose heart is doubly cold;
For in the time of sun and in the cold,
She casts an image for me like a woman
Who took her shaping finely out of rock
At the hand of him who's best at carving rock.

   And I, whose steadfastness is more than rock
Obeying you through beauty of a woman,
I bear the marks in secret of that rock
With which you struck, as if I were a rock
That irked your going for too long a time,
Such that it reached my heart, where I am rock.
   And never will my fingers hold that rock
Which by reflected or by inner light
Contains sufficient power or such light
That I might be delivered of this rock
And she no longer draw me with her cold
There where stone-maker Death will leave me cold.

   My Lord, you know that in the grip of cold
Water compacts into transparent rock
Under the north whose master is great cold,
And always into substances of cold
The air is so transformed, that water's woman
And mistress there by agency of cold;

così dinanzi dal sembiante freddo
mi ghiaccia sopra il sangue d'ogne tempo,
e quel pensiero che m'accorcia il tempo
mi si converte tutto in corpo freddo,
che m'esce poi per mezzo de la luce
là ond'entrò la dispietata luce.

In lei s'accoglie d'ogni bieltà luce;
così di tutta crudeltate il freddo
le corre al core, ove non va tua luce:
per che ne li occhi sì bella mi luce
quando la miro, ch'io la veggio in petra,
e po' in ogni altro ov'io volga mia luce.
Da li occhi suoi mi ven la dolce luce
che mi fa non caler d'ogn'altra donna:
così foss'ella più pietosa donna
ver me, che chiamo di notte e di luce,
solo per lei servire, e luogo e tempo!
Né per altro disio viver gran tempo.

Però, vertù che se' prima che tempo,
prima che moto o che sensibil luce,
increscati di me, c'ho sì mal tempo;
entrale in core omai, ché ben n'è tempo,
sì che per te se n'esca fuor lo freddo
che non mi lascia aver, com'altri, tempo:
ché se mi giunge lo tuo forte tempo
in tale stato, questa gentil petra
mi vedrà coricare in poca petra,
per non levarmi se non dopo il tempo,
quando vedrò se mai fu bella donna
nel mondo come questa acerba donna.

Thus, held before her face intent on cold,
I feel ice clog my blood at every time,
And that reflection which curtails my time
Has metamorphosed to incarnate cold
Which scatters tears where I receive the light
And once let in that unrelenting light.

In her amasses beauty all its light
So that all cruelty distilled to cold
Runs to her heart, where there can come no light;
And thus my eyes are doors to such a light
When I regard her, I see her stand in rock
And in all else where I go seeking light.
Her eyes impart to me that tender light
Which leaves me blind to any other woman—
And would she were in pity more a woman
Toward me, who ask from darkness and from light,
That I may serve her, only place and time!
For nothing else would I be long in Time.

And therefore, Power who precede all Time,
Precede all Motion and substantial Light,
Take pity on me, whose is so ill a time,
Enter her heart, for it is long since time,
So that by you may issue forth that cold
Which hinders me while others have their time;
If your full strength should come to me in time
As I am now, that shape of noble rock
Will see me make my bed inside the rock
With no arising till the end of time,
When all will know if earth bore ever woman
So lovely as this cruel unripened woman.

179

Canzone, io porto ne la mente donna
tal, che, con tutto ch'ella mi sia petra,
mi dà baldanza, ond'ogni uom mi par freddo:
sì ch'io ardisco a far per questo freddo
la novità che per tua forma luce,
che non fu mai pensata in alcun tempo.

My song, I carry in my thoughts a woman
Such, that although to me she be like rock,
She gives me heart, whence other men seem cold,
And I dare undertake, though she be cold,
The novelty which fills your form with light
And none conceived or wrought before this time.

Così nel mio parlar voglio esser aspro
com'è ne li atti questa bella petra,
la quale ognora impetra
maggior durezza e più natura cruda,
 e veste sua persona d'un dïaspro
tal, che per lui, o perch'ella s'arretra,
non esce di faretra
saetta che già mai la colga ignuda:
 ed ella ancide, e non val ch'om si chiuda
né si dilunghi da' colpi mortali,
che, com'avesser ali,
giungono altrui e spezzan ciascun'arme;
sì ch'io non so da lei né posso atarme.

 Non trovo scudo ch'ella non mi spezzi
né loco che dal suo viso m'asconda;
ché, come fior di fronda,
così de la mia mente tien la cima.
 Cotanto del mio mal par che si prezzi
quanto legno di mar che non lieva onda;
e 'l peso che m'affonda
è tal che non potrebbe adequar rima.
 Ahi angosciosa e dispietata lima
che sordamente la mia vita scemi,
perché non ti ritemi
sì di rodermi il core a scorza a scorza,
com'io di dire altrui chi ti dà forza?

 Ché più mi triema il cor qualora io penso
di lei in parte ov'altri li occhi induca,
per tema non traluca
lo mio penser di fuor sì che si scopra,

Now would I file my speech into a rasp
As harsh as that fair stone-maid in her acts,
She who hourly contracts
More obduracy and plays a crueller part,
   Whose body jasper wraps in such a grasp
That, turned by it or bent on day-old tracks,
No quiver here but lacks
Arrow to pierce the stone and find her heart.
   She kills: let no one trust to armorer's art
Or speed of foot against the bow she strings,
For each, as if on wings,
Each shot goes home, and so transfixed am I,
I cannot ward them off, nor dare to try.

   I have no armor that she cannot split,
Nor hiding-place, though I should go and dig;
A flower atop its twig,
She crowns my thoughts for better and for worse;
   As for my anguish, she responds to it
As if I were calm seas, and she a brig;
The load is far too big
I sink beneath to fit into my verse.
   You gnawing teeth, you cankers that I nurse,
Who eat my life and will not heed my pain,
Why can you not abstain
From gouging through my heart-flesh, layer by layer,
As I from naming her who set you there?

   More trembling takes my heart when I recall
Her where keen eyes may fall upon my face,
In fear lest there they trace
Light that betrays the light within my brain,

ch'io non fo de la morte, che ogni senso
co li denti d'Amor già mi manduca;
ciò è che 'l pensier bruca
la lor vertù, sì che n'allenta l'opra.
   E' m'ha percosso in terra, e stammi sopra
con quella spada ond'elli ancise Dido,
Amore, a cui io grido
merzé chiamando, e umilmente il priego;
ed el d'ogni merzé par messo al niego.

   Egli alza ad ora ad or la mano, e sfida
la debole mia vita, esto perverso,
che disteso a riverso
mi tiene in terra d'ogni guizzo stanco:
   allor mi surgon ne la mente strida;
e 'l sangue, ch'è per le vene disperso,
fuggendo corre verso
lo cor, che 'l chiama; ond'io rimango bianco.
   Elli mi fiede sotto il braccio manco
sì forte, che 'l dolor nel cor rimbalza:
allor dico: 'S'elli alza
un'altra volta, Morte m'avrà chiuso
prima che 'l colpo sia disceso giuso.'

   Così vedess'io lui fender per mezzo
lo core a la crudele che 'l mio squatra!
poi non mi sarebb'atra
la morte, ov'io per sua bellezza corro:
   ché tanto dà nel sol quanto nel rezzo
questa scherana micidiale e latra.
Omè, perché non latra
per me, com'io per lei, nel caldo borro?

Than when I think of death, though death through all
My senses follows Love who gnaws each place
With thoughts which give no grace,
And feeling slows and slackens in their train.
  He strikes me down and holds his sword of pain
Suspended, that sword which gave Queen Dido death,
Love's self, on whom my breath
Is spent in crying "Mercy," to whom I pray:
But he is one that mercy cannot sway.

  Time and again he lifts his hand and tries
My flagging strength, and his malignities
Permit me little ease
Pinned to the ground, too tired to twist and bite;
  Then all my thoughts are stricken into cries,
My blood, which knew its paths and their degrees,
Thrown in disorder flees
To my heart which summons it, and I turn white.
  He wounds me under the left arm with his right
So deeply, my heart brims anguish like a cup,
And then I say, "Lift up
Your hand once more, my Lord, death will step in
Before the blow you threaten breaks the skin."

  Would I might see him halve it with his blade,
That cruel one's heart who makes my heart her mark!
Then death would not be dark
To me, though for her sake I run to be his
  Whose work she does as much in sun as shade,
This homicide who leaves men lying stark.
Ah, and why will she not bark
For me, as I for her, in the red abyss?

ché tosto griderei: 'Io vi soccorro';
e fare' l volentier, sì come quelli
che ne' biondi capelli
ch'Amor per consumarmi increspa e dora
metterei mano, e piacere'le allora.

S'io avessi le belle trecce prese,
che fatte son per me scudiscio e ferza,
pigliandole anzi terza,
con esse passerei vespero e squille:
    e non sarei pietoso né cortese,
anzi farei com'orso quando scherza;
e se Amor me ne sferza,
io mi vendicherei di più di mille.
    Ancor ne li occhi, ond'escon le faville
che m'infiammano il cor, ch'io porto anciso,
guarderei presso e fiso,
per vendicar lo fuggir che mi face;
e poi le renderei con amor pace.

Canzon, vatene dritto a quella donna
che m'ha ferito il core e che m'invola
quello ond'io ho più gola,
e dàlle per lo cor d'una saetta:
ché bell'onor s'acquista in far vendetta.

Then I'd quickly cry, "Look! help is near," and this
I'd do with pleasure, like certain others, hold
Hair in long hanks of gold
(To which, that I may die, Love gives the curl)
Between these fingers, and so would please my girl.

Give me those tresses—so thick they fall, so bright—
Which to my hurt have served as scourge and thong,
From start of matin-song
I'll hold them fast till after evening choir;
    And she'd not find me gentle or polite
When I play bear, a playful bear, but strong;
And though Love's whipped me long,
A thousand strokes I'd give her, and not tire.
    Then in her eyes, whence came those stars of fire
At which my heart took flame, that now is dead,
I'd gaze, head close to head,
To pay her out for that escape and this;
And last, with love, I'd offer armistice.

My song, go straight up to that certain lady
Who pierced my heart and yet will not concede
What I in hunger need,
And send an arrow home into her breast:
For great revenge, great honor crowns one's quest.

Tre donne intorno al cor mi son venute,
e seggonsi di fore;
ché dentro siede Amore,
lo quale è in segnoria de la mia vita.
 Tanto son belle e di tanta vertute,
che 'l possente segnore,
dico quel ch'è nel core,
a pena del parlar di lor s'aita.
 Ciascuna par dolente e sbigottita,
come persona discacciata e stanca,
cui tutta gente manca
e cui vertute né beltà non vale.
Tempo fu già nel quale,
secondo il lor parlar, furon dilette;
or sono a tutti in ira ed in non cale.
Queste così solette
venute son come a casa d'amico;
ché sanno ben che dentro è quel ch'io dico.

 Dolesi l'una con parole molto,
e 'n su la man si posa
come succisa rosa:
il nudo braccio, di dolor colonna,
 sente l'oraggio che cade dal volto;
l'altra man tiene ascosa
la faccia lagrimosa:
discinta e scalza, e sol di sé par donna.
 Come Amor prima per la rotta gonna
la vide in parte che il tacere è bello,
egli, pietoso e fello,
di lei e del dolor fece dimanda.

81

Around my heart, as if they went to earth,
Three women sit, for in
It Love has always been,
He who has government of all my days.
   So beautiful these three, and such their worth,
That mighty lord of men
Who makes my heart his den,
Struck at their plight, for long can shape no phrase.
   They sit with grief, bewildered, in a daze,
Like people hounded forth and hunger-pale
Who see their friends all fail
And in whom worth and beauty win no stay.
There was a time, they say,
A time not long ago, they gave delight;
Now faces frown at them, or look away.
By lonely roads, at night,
They seek my house as if it were a friend's,
For well they know the dweller whom it tends.

   With long complaint one wept for their disgrace
While right hand cradled head
Like rose plucked from its bed
(The naked arm, white hand, grief's capital,
Swayed in the storm that fell from her stricken face),
   And with her left she hid
Those features tears undid,
Barefoot and beltless, way-worn but lady still.
   When first (what skirts in tatters covered ill)
Love saw those parts no decent man will name,
In anger and in shame
He asked her who she was and why she wept;

'Oh di pochi vivanda',
rispose in voce con sospiri mista,
'nostra natura qui a te ci manda:
io, che son la più trista,
son suora a la tua madre, e son Drittura;
povera, vedi, a panni ed a cintura.'

    Poi che fatta si fu palese e conta,
doglia e vergogna prese
lo mio segnore, e chiese
chi fosser l'altre due ch'eran con lei.
    E questa, ch'era sì di pianger pronta,
tosto che lui intese,
più nel dolor s'accese,
dicendo: 'A te non duol de gli occhi miei?'
    Poi cominciò: 'Sì come saper dei,
di fonte nasce il Nilo picciol fiume
quivi dove 'l gran lume
toglie a la terra del vinco la fronda:
sovra la vergin onda
generai io costei che m'è da lato
e che s'asciuga con la treccia bionda.
Questo mio bel portato,
mirando sé ne la chiara fontana,
generò questa che m'è più lontana.'

    Fenno i sospiri Amore un poco tardo;
e poi con gli occhi molli,
che prima furon folli,
salutò le germane sconsolate.
    E poi che prese l'uno e l'altro dardo,
disse: 'Drizzate i colli:
ecco l'armi ch'io volli;
per non usar, vedete, son turbate.

"O bread that few accept,"
She said, and deep-drawn sighs were interspersed,
"Our kinship is the reason that we came,
For I, in sorrow first,
Am Justice, and my sister gave you birth—
Though as you see, my clothes are of small worth."

Now she had made her birth and nature clear,
Both shame and sorrow laid
Hold of my lord, who prayed
She name the two who sat there at her side;
   And she who was so quick with tear on tear,
Soon as she understood,
Let grief burn what it would,
Crying, "These eyes bring you no pain?" replied:
   "As you must know, where Adam took his bride,
A spring engenders Nile step-wide and shy;
At noon the heavens' bright eye
Contracts the willow-shade till earth is bare.
Beside the pure wave there,
Her at my side I brought forth to our line
Who dries her eyelids now with yellow hair.
This lovely child of mine
Gazed in the liquid mirror, and approved,
And bore that other sitting once removed."

Although sighs make it hard for him to start,
Eyes swimming and distraught,
Unseeing while untaught,
Love greets his kindred where they sit forlorn,
   And taking up this gold, that leaden dart,
Begins, "Lift up your thought,
Behold the arms I sought,
Look how disuse defiles them, though unworn.

Larghezza e Temperanza e l'altre nate
del nostro sangue mendicando vanno.
Però, se questo è danno,
piangano gli occhi e dolgasi la bocca
de li uomini a cui tocca,
che sono a' raggi di cotal ciel giunti;
non noi, che semo de l'etterna rocca:
ché, se noi siamo or punti,
noi pur saremo, e pur tornerà gente
che questo dardo farà star lucente.'

E io, che ascolto nel parlar divino
consolarsi e dolersi
così alti dispersi,
l'essilio che m'è dato, onor mi tegno:
ché, se giudizio o forza di destino
vuol pur che il mondo versi
i bianchi fiori in persi,
cader co' buoni è pur di lode degno.
E se non che de gli occhi miei 'l bel segno
per lontananza m'è tolto dal viso,
che m'have in foco miso,
lieve mi conterei ciò che m'è grave.
Ma questo foco m'have
già consumato sì l'ossa e la polpa
che Morte al petto m'ha posto la chiave.
Onde, s'io ebbi colpa,
più lune ha volto il sol poi che fu spenta,
se colpa muore perché l'uom si penta.

Canzone, a' panni tuoi non ponga uom mano,
per veder quel che bella donna chiude:
bastin le parti nude;
lo dolce pome a tutta gente niega,
per cui ciascun man piega.

Restraint and Open-Hand and others born
Of our high blood extend a beggar's bowl;
But though we count the toll,
Let mankind shed the tears, let mankind groan
And suffer all alone
From hostile stars that lour in the north—
Our house is built of everlasting stone,
And though they drive us forth,
We will endure, and last a people come
Who'll scour each dart till it shine like the sun."

And I, who hear in their angelic speech
Wanderers from such a height
Find joy and pain in sight,
The exile I must bear, honor I call:
For though God's will or vicar Fortune teach
Earth's valley how to blight
White blooms to black as night,
It still is best to join the good, and fall.
If that fair goal to which my eyes are thrall
Were not removed where sight cannot aspire
(Which sets my heart on fire),
I'd think no burden all that burdens me.
But love's intensity
Has made such havoc of my flesh and bone,
Into my breastlock Death has thrust his key.
Say I'd a fault to own—
For months the sun has looked on innocence
If guilt is canceled when a man repents.

My song, let none set fingers to your dress
To see those parts which lovely women hide,
Suffice what lies outside,
Deny to all the apple and its sweets
Though hands be at your pleats;

Ma s'elli avvien che tu alcun mai truovi
amico di virtù, ed e' ti priega,
fatti di color novi,
poi li ti mostra; e 'l fior, ch'è bel di fori,
fa' disïar ne li amorosi cori.

Canzone, uccella con le bianche penne;
canzone, caccia con li neri veltri,
che fuggir mi convenne,
ma far mi poterian di pace dono.
Però nol fan che non san quel che sono:
camera di perdon savio uom non serra,
ché 'l perdonare è bel vincer di guerra.

But if it ever chance, someday, that you
Discover virtue's friend, and he entreats,
Make all your colors new,
Then show yourself—so fair its outer parts,
Your bloom will stir desire in loving hearts.

   My song, go stoop with the snowy hawks for me,
Go run the trails, my song, with the sable hounds
Which I have had to flee,
Though peace is theirs and what they will they can—
They will not, for they know not what I am:
The wise will keep forgiveness' door ajar,
Knowing forgiveness bears the palm in war.

Se vedi li occhi miei di pianger vaghi
per novella pietà che 'l cor mi strugge,
per lei ti priego che da te non fugge,
Signor, che tu di tal piacere i svaghi;

con la tua dritta man, cioè, che paghi
chi la giustizia uccide e poi rifugge
al gran tiranno, del cui tosco sugge
ch'elli ha già sparto e vuol che 'l mondo allaghi;

e messo ha di paura tanto gelo
nel cor de' tuo' fedei che ciascun tace.
Ma tu, foco d'amor, lume del cielo,

questa vertù che nuda e fredda giace,
levala su vestita del tuo velo,
ché sanza lei non è in terra pace.

82

If you have seen my eyes desiring tears
In recent pain from which my heart still shrinks,
I pray by her to whom you have close links,
Give them such joy, Lord, suffering disappears:

Touch with your right hand, the hand that sears,
Whoever murders justice and then sinks
To the great tyrant, and of his poison drinks
Which he has loosed to drown all fruitful ears.

For he has fastened such congealing fright
Upon your faithful hearts that all are dumb:
But you, the Fire of Love and Heaven's Light,

That virtue which lies naked here and numb,
Lift her up clothed in your celestial white,
For where she's absent, peace can never come.

Doglia mi reca ne lo core ardire
a voler ch'è di veritate amico;
però, donne, s'io dico
parole quasi contra a tutta gente,
non vi maravigliate,
    ma conoscete il vil vostro disire:
ché la beltà ch'Amore in voi consente,
a vertù solamente
formata fu dal suo decreto antico,
contra 'l qual voi fallate.
    Io dico a voi che siete innamorate
che, se vertute a noi
fu data, e beltà a voi,
e a costui di due potere un fare,
voi non dovreste amare,
ma coprir quanto di biltà v'è dato,
poi che non c'è vertù, ch'era suo segno.
Lasso, a che dicer vegno?
Dico che bel disdegno
sarebbe in donna, di ragion laudato,
partir beltà da sé per suo commiato.

    Omo da sé vertù fatto ha lontana;
omo no, mala bestia ch'om simiglia.
O Deo, qual maraviglia
voler cadere in servo di signore,
o ver di vita in morte!
    Vertute, al suo fattor sempre sottana,
lui obedisce e lui acquista onore,
donne, tanto che Amore
la segna d'eccellente sua famiglia
ne la beata corte:

Emboldening pain has set my heart on fire
To speak a word that truth would call its friend.
So ladies, if I offend
Against all but a few by speaking home,
Please do not be dismayed,
  But grasp how baseness poisons your desire.
The beauty Love has suffered you to own
For virtue's work alone
Was formed by law he wrought and will defend,
The which you have betrayed.
  I say to you, where pacts of love are made,
If yours are beauty's powers
And virtue should be ours
And his the art to make of two things one,
You must give love to none
But hide the beauty sent at his decree,
Since here's no virtue, and virtue was its aim.
Alas, what says my shame?
One could not but acclaim
A woman for her brave contempt if she
Herself dismissed her beauty willingly.

  Man beholds virtue yet can still forsake her:
Not man, but some vile beast which mimics man.
O God, who'd understand
This fall they hunger for from lord to slave,
From life to life's grim mate?
  Virtue, a sure lieutenant to her maker,
Obeys his will and graces his conclave
So well, ladies, Love gave
His sign she ranks above the best who stand
Where he keeps blissful state:

lietamente esce da le belle porte,
a la sua donna torna;
lieta va e soggiorna,
lietamente ovra suo gran vassallaggio;
per lo corto vïaggio
conserva, adorna, accresce ciò che trova;
Morte repugna sì che lei non cura.
O cara ancella e pura,
colt'hai nel ciel misura;
tu sola fai segnore, e quest'è prova
che tu se' possession che sempre giova.

Servo non di signor, ma di vil servo
si fa chi da cotal serva si scosta.
Vedete quanto costa,
se ragionate l'uno e l'altro danno,
a chi da lei si svia:
questo servo signor tant'è protervo,
che gli occhi ch'a la mente lume fanno
chiusi per lui si stanno,
sì che gir ne convene a colui posta,
ch'adocchia pur follia.
Ma perché lo meo dire util vi sia,
discenderò del tutto
in parte, ed in costrutto
più lieve, sì che men grave s'intenda:
ché rado sotto benda
parola oscura giugne ad intelletto;
per che parlar con voi si vole aperto:
ma questo vo' per merto,
per voi, non per me certo,
ch'abbiate a vil ciascuno e a dispetto,
ché simiglianza fa nascer diletto.

Joyfully she issues from the lovely gate,
Seeks where her lady bides,
In joy remains or rides,
Joyfully performs a vassal's mission though
Aware she soon must go,
Preserves, adorns, and furthers all she cures:
Traffic with Death was never to her taste.
Maidservant sweet and chaste,
With heaven's Measure graced,
Alone you make us lords, and this insures
That you are one possession that endures.

No lord's retainer, but a filthy slave's,
Is he who thrusts that serving-maid aside.
You see what costs abide
(Were you to calculate his double load)
For him who leaves her grace.
    This haughty slave and master so behaves,
Those eyes through which our mind's light all has flowed
Are shut, and down the road
We stumble, bound to him as guide
Who ogles folly's face.
    But that my words may better serve your case,
I'll try another key
And speak less generally
In terms at grasping which no woman quails—
For rarely under veils
Will darkling verses lead the mind to light,
So I'll speak plainly to your sisterhood.
But please, in gratitude,
For your, not my, own good,
Treat men as vile and hold them in despite—
Unless you're like them, they give no delight.

Chi è servo è come quello ch'è seguace
ratto a segnore, e non sa dove vada,
per dolorosa strada;
come l'avaro seguitando avere,
ch'a tutti segnoreggia.
Corre l'avaro, ma più fugge pace:
oh mente cieca, che non pò vedere
lo suo folle volere
che 'l numero, ch'ognora a passar bada,
che 'nfinito vaneggia!
Ecco giunta colei che ne pareggia:
dimmi, che hai tu fatto,
cieco avaro disfatto?
Rispondimi, se puoi, altro che 'Nulla'.
Maladetta tua culla,
che lusingò cotanti sonni invano!
Maladetto lo tuo perduto pane,
che non si perde al cane!
ché da sera e da mane
hai raunato e stretto ad ambo mano
ciò che sì tosto si rifà lontano.

Come con dismisura si rauna,
così con dismisura si distringe:
questo è quello che pinge
molti in servaggio; e s'alcun si difende,
non è sanza gran briga.
Morte, che fai? che fai, fera Fortuna,
che non solvete quel che non si spende?
se 'l fate, a cui si rende?
Non so, poscia che tal cerchio ne cinge
che di là su ne riga.
Colpa è de la ragion che nol gastiga.
Se vol dire 'I' son presa',

These slaves are like those who for good and ill
Follow their lord along a way of pain
Whose goal is far from plain;
Like the grey miser fawning at wealth's heels,
On which all men attend.
    The miser runs but peace runs faster still.
Blind thought! where folly put such lasting seals
Volition never deals
Except with sums at whose increase you'll strain
Forever, to no end!
    Behold, he's come who equalizes men:
Tell me, what did you do,
Blind miser, now you're through?
Nothing to say to me but, "Not a thing"?
Cursed be your cradling
Which vainly rocked so many nights to sleep!
Cursed be that waste of good white loaves you ate—
Would dogs had had your plate!
For early, yes, and late,
From right and left you've scraped into a heap
What quickly slips away and none can keep.

    Beyond all measure, wealth can be amassed
And then beyond all measure lie unspent:
And this is what has sent
Many to bondage; if some escape this doom,
It's not without a fight.
    Fortune and Death, you see how he holds fast?
Will you not liquidate this golden tomb?
Yet if you did, for whom?
No one—the stars that hem us in prevent
Our rising to the light—
    Reason's to blame, which will not put this right.
The reason? "I'm in jail."

ah com poca difesa
mostra segnore a cui servo sormonta!
Qui si raddoppia l'onta,
se ben si guarda là dov'io addito,
falsi animali, a voi ed altrui crudi,
che vedete gir nudi
per colli e per paludi
omini innanzi cui vizio è fuggito,
e voi tenete vil fango vestito.

    Fassi dinanzi da l'avaro volto
vertù, che i suoi nimici a pace invita,
con matera pulita,
per allettarlo a sé; ma poco vale,
ché sempre fugge l'esca.
    Poi che girato l'ha chiamando molto,
gitta 'l pasto ver lui, tanto glien cale;
ma quei non v'apre l'ale:
e se pur vene quand'ell'è partita,
tanto par che li 'ncresca
    come ciò possa dar, sì che non esca
dal benefizio loda.
I' vo' che ciascun m'oda:
chi con tardare, e chi con vana vista,
chi con sembianza trista,
volge il donare in vender tanto caro
quanto sa sol chi tal compera paga.
Volete udir se piaga?
Tanto chi prende smaga,
che 'l negar poscia non li pare amaro.
Così altrui e sé concia l'avaro.

    Disvelato v'ho, donne, in alcun membro
la viltà de la gente che vi mira,
perché l'aggiate in ira;

But how can it avail
A lord to tell us that his slave's in charge?
And for disgrace writ large,
Just fix your eyes where I direct my fire,
You self-made beasts, whose sufferings we must share:
Through hills and marshes fare
Good men with nothing to wear
Before whom vice has fled, while rich attire
Has gone to waste in tricking out your mire.

The miser watches virtue come to him
To hold out peace, as she will to her foes,
With something else that throws
A light to catch his eye—but nothing brings
Him down to take the bait.
  She circles, crying, "Do let go that limb!"
And then she throws the dainty where he clings;
He'll still not spread his wings,
And if he takes the lure when virtue goes,
His terror is so great
  She'll charge him for it, none of us would rate
The action worth a word.
I hope you all have heard
Who with delay or a complacent face,
Or with an evil grace,
Turn gifts to purchases that come so dear
To those poor souls who owe you for their shirt.
You wonder, does it hurt?
Who takes must eat such dirt
Denial after seems not worth a tear:
Taker and stingy giver suffer here.

Ladies, from what I've told, you may surmise
The baseness of those men who stand at gaze—
I hope you'll loathe such praise;

ma troppo è più ancor quel che s'asconde
perché a dicerne è lado.
    In ciascun è di ciascun vizio assembro,
per che amistà nel mondo si confonde:
ché l'amorose fronde
di radice di ben altro ben tira,
poi sol simile è in grado.
    Vedete come conchiudendo vado:
che non dee creder quella
cui par bene esser bella,
esser amata da questi cotali;
che se beltà tra i mali
volemo annumerar, creder si pòne,
chiamando amore appetito di fera!
Oh cotal donna pera
che sua biltà dischiera
da natural bontà per tal cagione,
e crede amor fuor d'orto di ragione!

    Canzone, presso di qui è una donna
ch'è del nostro paese;
bella, saggia e cortese
la chiaman tutti, e neun se n'accorge
quando suo nome porge,
Bianca, Giovanna, Contessa chiamando:
a costei te ne va' chiusa ed onesta;
prima con lei t'arresta,
prima a lei manifesta
quel che tu se' e quel per ch'io ti mando;
poi seguirai secondo suo comando.

But much remains too ugly to be said
Or for your eyes to scan.
    In each a coil of each corruption lies,
And friendship in this world is nearly dead:
If love's leaves are to spread,
Good root and some good else must feed the sprays,
As only like things can.
    Now watch how I conclude what I began:
Who thinks that beauty should
Be numbered with what's good,
Let her beware the love of all this tribe;
Though if she will ascribe
Beauty to evil, let her heed their speech
And think that love's the hunger of a beast!
Oh may her life be short
Whose beauty bans from court
All native good, believing what some teach,
That love's run wild and out of reason's reach!

    My song, not far from here a lady dwells
Who shares birthplace with us:
"Fair," "wise," and "courteous"
All call her, yet they fail to realize
What her name signifies,
Saying BIANCA, GIOVANNA, and TESSA, too—
Discreet and modest, go now where she stands,
No halt till on her lands,
Deliver to those hands
What sort you are and what I trust to you
And then continue where she bids you to.

84a   (CINO DA PISTOIA)

Novellamente Amor mi giura e dice
d'una donna gentil, s'i' la riguardo,
che per vertù de lo su' novo sguardo
ella sarà del meo cor bëatrice.

Io c'ho provato po' come disdice,
quando vede imbastito lo suo dardo,
ciò che promette, a morte mi do tardo,
ch'i' non potrò contraffar la fenice.

S'io levo gli occhi, e del suo colpo perde
lo core mio quel poco che di vita
gli rimase d'un'altra sua ferita.

Che farò, Dante? ch'Amor pur m'invita,
e d'altra parte il tremor mi disperde
che peggio che lo scur non mi sia 'l verde.

84a

Just now, Love swore on oath that if I fix
Upon a certain face, my heart's reward
By virtue of that wonderful regard
Will be her gentle self as beatrix.

But I have some acquaintance with his tricks
(How, once he thinks he's got inside my guard,
He will renege) and feel it's rather hard
To have to die, seeing that I'm no phoenix.

If I looked up, his stroke would drain away
The little life my heart can realize
After the wound it took from other eyes.

Dante, what shall I do? "Look up!" Love cries,
But all the same, I tremble in dismay
Lest green should try me harder than does gray.

I'ho veduto già senza radice
legno ch'è per omor tanto gagliardo,
che que' che vide nel fiume lombardo
cader suo figlio, fronde fuor n'elice;

ma frutto no, però che 'l contradice
natura, ch'al difetto fa riguardo,
perché conosce che saria bugiardo
sapor non fatto da vera notrice.

Giovane donna a cotal guisa verde
talor per gli occhi sì dentro è gita
che tardi poi è stata la partita.

Periglio è grande in donna sì vestita:
però †lacontro† de la gente verde
parmi che la tua caccia [non] seguer de'.

84

I've seen the thing before, five times or six:
A fallen tree has so much sap aboard
That he whose son the fires of heaven scarred
And Po received can draw leaves from its sticks,

But never fruit, which Nature interdicts
Who knows to what extent the plant is marred
And that she'd end by having to discard
Fruitage in nursing which Earth did not mix.

A half-grown woman, green in just this way,
May reach, once she is seen, a place that lies
So far inside, she's slow to leave her prize.

From women dressed in green great perils rise:
Therefore you'll find it safer, I should say,
To drop this hunt before she turns at bay.

85

Perch'io non trovo chi meco ragioni
del signor a cui siete voi ed io,
conviemmi sodisfare al gran disio
ch'i'ho di dire i pensamenti boni.

Null'altra cosa appo voi m'accagioni
del lungo e del noioso tacer mio
se non il loco ov'i' son, ch'è sì rio
che 'l ben non trova chi albergo li doni.

Donna non ci ha ch'Amor le venga al volto,
né omo ancora che per lui sospiri;
e chi 'l facesse qua sarebbe stolto.

Oh, messer Cin, come 'l tempo è rivolto
a danno nostro e de li nostri diri,
da po' che 'l ben è sì poco ricolto!

85

I find none here to reason properly
Of him whom we acknowledge, you and I,
So there is only verse to satisfy
My wish to tell good thoughts which come to me.

Let nothing bear responsibility
For these long tedious months without reply
Except the place I live, that's such a sty
Good finds no one to give him hostelry:

No woman here in whose face Love is read
Nor man who weeps in prayer for Love's sight—
Who did, would find he's mocked upon that head.

O messer Cino, how the years have led
Us to great loss, and most in what we write,
Since Good went begging for his board and bed!

85a   (CINO DA PISTOIA)

Dante, i' non so in qual albergo soni
lo ben, ch'è da ciascun messo in oblio:
è sì gran tempo che di qua fuggio
che del contraro son nati li troni;

e per le varïate condizioni
chi 'l ben tacesse, non risponde al fio:
lo ben sa' tu che predicava Iddio,
e nol tacea nel regno de' dimoni.

Dunque, s'al ben ciascun ostello è tolto
nel mondo, in ogni parte ove ti giri,
vuoli tu anco far dispiacer molto?

Diletto frate mio, di pene involto,
merzé, per quella donna che tu miri,
d'opra non star, se di fé non se' sciolto.

Dante, I know not in what hostelry
Goodness is heard, who's lost his last ally;
Such weather has set in, Good had to fly—
It thunders the reverse of what should be.

Yet, though our circumstances alter, he
Who has no word for Good lets duty die:
You know that Christ preached good beneath the sky,
And even down in hell his speech was free.

Therefore, if Good has neither barn nor shed
To shelter in, no matter where you light,
Why would you heap more trouble on his head?

Beloved brother mine, to suffering wed,
I pray, by her in whom you find the light,
Cease not from works, if faith be not yet dead.

86a   (CINO DA PISTOIA)

Dante, quando per caso s'abbandona
lo disio amoroso de la speme
che nascer fanno gli occhi del bel seme
di quel piacer che dentro si ragiona,

i' dico, poi se morte le perdona
e Amore tienla più de le due estreme,
che l'alma sola, la qual più non teme,
si può ben trasformar d'altra persona.

E ciò mi fa dir quella ch'è maestra
di tutte cose, per quel ch'i' sent'anco
entrato, lasso, per la mia fenestra.

Ma prima che m'uccida il nero e il bianco,
da te, che se' istato dentro ed extra,
vorre' saper se 'l mi' creder è manco.

86a

If true desire which Love has set in train,
Dante, perchance give up the hopeful dreams
Our eyes educe from that fair seed which teems
With pleasures for our thoughts to entertain,

And if, I say, our soul can bear the strain
And Love controls her, not the two extremes,
Then free of fear the soul herself, one deems,
Can take another person as her aim.

Experience makes me say these words, the crowned
Queen of all things, for Love has pitched his tent
Once more behind where my two windows round.

The black and white will kill me—first, consent,
Since you've been in and out, that you'll expound
All imperfections in my argument.

Io sono stato con Amore insieme
da la circulazion del sol mia nona,
e so com'egli affrena e come sprona,
e come sotto lui si ride e geme.

Chi ragione o virtù contra gli sprieme,
fa come que' che 'n la tempesta sona,
credendo far colà dove si tona
esser le guerre de' vapori sceme.

Però nel cerchio de la sua palestra
liber arbitrio già mai non fu franco,
sì che consiglio invan vi si balestra.

Ben può con nuovi spron punger lo fianco,
e qual che sia 'l piacer ch'ora n'addestra,
seguitar si convien, se l'altro è stanco.

I have stood now in the brightness of Love's beams
Since I beheld my ninth year on its wane
And know how he will handle spur and rein
And how both tears and laughter are his themes.

Who pleads good sense and virtue where he gleams
Apes him who when the storms beat at his brain
Cries out and hopes where thunders mount and reign
To dam embattled vapors in their streams.

Within the circuit of this wrestling-ground
Free will has never won enfranchisement
And wisdom's darts have vainly sought to wound.

To ply new spurs may sometimes suit his bent:
Whatever the fair face which he has found,
Follow we must, once other charms are spent.

87a   (CINO DA PISTOIA)

Cercando di trovar minera in oro
di quel valor cui gentilezza inchina,
punto m'ha 'l cor, marchese, mala spina,
in guisa che, versando il sangue, i' moro.

E più per quel ched i' non trovo ploro
che per la vita natural che fina:
cotal pianeta, lasso, mi destina
che dov'io perdo volentier dimoro.

E più le pene mie vi farie conte,
se non ched i' non vo' che troppa gioia
vo' concepiate di ciò che m'è noia.

Ben poria il mio segnor, anzi ch'io moia,
far convertir in oro duro monte,
c'ha fatto già di marmo nascer fonte.

87a

Seeking an ore in Love's profoundest mine
Whose golden worth no gentle man would scorn,
My heart was pricked, Marquis, by "evilthorn"
And now from loss of blood I droop and pine.

I shed more tears for what I cannot find
Than for my body's life that's long outworn:
The stars, alas, ordained when I was born
That I agree to stay where I decline.

To you my pains would be more fully shown
If I'd no fear that you would apprehend
Too great a joy in that to which I bend.

My lord could easily, before my end,
Transform to gold this barren hill of stone
Who made from marble living waters foam.

87

Degno fa voi trovare ogni tesoro
la voce vostra sì dolce e latina,
ma volgibile cor ven disvicina,
ove stecco d'Amor mai non fé foro.

Io che trafitto sono in ogni poro
del prun che con sospir si medicina,
pur trovo la minera in cui s'affina
quella virtù per cui mi discoloro.

Non è colpa del sol se l'orba fronte
nol vede quando scende e quando poia,
ma de la condizion malvagia e croia.

S'i' vi vedesse uscir de gli occhi ploia
per prova fare a le parole conte,
non mi porreste di sospetto in ponte.

87

That your sweet voice could only be a sign
That you deserve all wealth, I would have sworn;
A fickle heart has left your search forlorn,
For Love has never touched you with keen spine.

For all my wounds, whose only anodyne
Is sighs that heal what spiny Love has torn,
I still find ore in which the gold is borne
That drains its color from this face of mine.

Who'd blame the sun if brow of eyeless bone
Can't see him rise and can't see him descend,
And not its evil state these ills attend?

Though I had seen your eyes drop rain, my friend,
To vouch for what your clever words bemoan,
You'd not have touched the doubts your deeds have sown.

Io mi credea del tutto esser partito
da queste nostre rime, messer Cino,
ché si conviene omai altro cammino
a la mia nave più lungi dal lito:

ma perch'i'ho di voi più volte udito
che pigliar vi lasciate a ogni uncino,
piacemi di prestare un pocolino
a questa penna lo stancato dito.

Chi s'innamora sì come voi fate,
or qua or là, e sé lega e dissolve,
mostra ch'Amor leggermente il saetti.

Però, se leggier cor così vi vole,
priego che con vertù il correggiate,
sì che s'accordi i fatti a' dolci detti.

88

I thought that I was done with all the store
Of verses, messer Cino, we have made,
For it would seem another course is laid
For your friend's ship as it moves out from shore;

But since I've heard so many times before
That you will dance to any tune that's played,
It is my pleasure briefly to persuade
This weary hand to take up pen once more.

Who falls in love as you are wont to do,
Now here, now there, first seeks, then severs ties—
Love spares his thoughts and wounds his flesh instead.

And so, if fickle heart controls your eyes,
I pray that virtue mend this fault in you
And sweet deeds answer what is sweetly said.

88a   (CINO DA PISTOIA)

Poi ch'i' fu', Dante, dal mio natal sito
fatto per greve essilio pellegrino
e lontanato dal piacer più fino
che mai formasse il Piacer infinito,

io son piangendo per lo mondo gito
sdegnato del morir come meschino;
e s'ho trovato a lui simil vicino,
dett'ho che questi m'ha lo cor ferito.

Né da le prime braccia dispietate,
onde 'l fermato disperar m'assolve,
son mosso perch'aiuto non aspetti;

ch'un piacer sempre me lega ed involve,
il qual conven che a simil di beltate
in molte donne sparte mi diletti.

88a

Driven, Dante, from native roof and door
At exile's hands to ply a pilgrim's trade
And far removed from beauty best assayed
Of all that endless Beauty ever bore,

Wandering the world I've wept my two eyes sore
Disdained by death like cripple asking aid,
And if I've found her likeness where I've strayed,
I've written how it struck to my heart's core.

Those first cruel arms I swore allegiance to
(Though firm despair permits a bond's demise
And I am past despair) I've never fled.

One beauty always holds me as its prize,
And thus it's right, where beauty's like shines through,
In women severally delight be fed.

Amor, da che convien pur ch'io mi doglia
perché la gente m'oda,
e mostri me d'ogni vertute spento,
  dammi savere a pianger come voglia,
sì che 'l duol che si snoda
portin le mie parole com'io 'l sento.
  Tu vo' ch'io muoia, e io ne son contento:
ma chi mi scuserà, s'io non so dire
ciò che mi fai sentire?
chi crederà ch'io sia omai sì colto?
E se mi dai parlar quanto tormento,
fa', signor mio, che innanzi al mio morire
questa rëa per me nol possa udire:
ché, se intendesse ciò che dentro ascolto,
pietà faria men bello il suo bel volto.

  Io non posso fuggir ch'ella non vegna
ne l'imagine mia,
se non come il pensier che la vi mena.
  L'anima folle, che al suo mal s'ingegna,
com'ella è bella e ria,
così dipinge, e forma la sua pena:
  poi la riguarda, e quando ella è ben piena
del gran disio che de li occhi le tira,
incontro a sé s'adira,
c'ha fatto il foco ond'ella trista incende.
Quale argomento di ragion raffrena,
ove tanta tempesta in me si gira?
L'angoscia, che non cape dentro, spira
fuor de la bocca sì ch'ella s'intende,
e anche a li occhi lor merito rende.

Love, against whom I must speak my sorrow's fill
To win all people's ears
And show them I am at my tether's end,
    Give me the skill for weeping with the will,
That pain which falls in tears
May find the words to speak as I intend.
    You wish my death and I'll bear what you send:
But who'll forgive me if I have not said
What path you make me tread?
And who'll believe the harness that I wear?
Granting me speech of pain which makes me bend,
Grant too, my lord, before I be quite dead,
She without pity may not hear how I've sped:
For if she knew what voice my heart must bear,
Pity would make her fair aspect less fair.

    I cannot flee her so she does not press
Into my imagery,
No more than thought which led her to my brain.
    My maddened soul, to aggravate distress,
Spiteful and fair to see
Depicts my foe and incarnates its pain;
    Then looks at her, and being full each vein
With strong desire which rises from those eyes,
To self-accusing flies—
The fire that burns in it was self-incurred.
On what pretext can reason seize the reins
When such a tempest rules my inner skies?
Anguish that will not rest within me cries
At my mouth with sighs and groans until it's heard
And my eyes pay for what their roving stirred.

La nimica figura, che rimane
vittorïosa e fera
e signoreggia la vertù che vole,
    vaga di se medesma andar mi fane
colà dov'ella è vera,
come simile a simil correr sòle.
    Ben conosco che va la neve al sole,
ma più non posso: fo come colui
che, nel podere altrui,
va co' suoi piedi al loco ov'egli è morto.
Quando son presso, parmi udir parole
dicer: 'Vie via vedrai morir costui!'
Allor mi volgo per veder a cui
mi raccomandi; e 'ntanto sono scorto
da li occhi che m'ancidono a gran torto.

    Qual io divegno sì feruto, Amore,
sailo tu, e non io,
che rimani a veder me sanza vita;
    e se l'anima torna poscia al core,
ignoranza ed oblio
stato è con lei, mentre ch'ella è partita.
    Com'io risurgo, e miro la ferita
che mi disfece quand'io fui percosso,
confortar non mi posso
sì ch'io non triemi tutto di paura.
E mostra poi la faccia scolorita
qual fu quel trono che mi giunse a dosso;
che se con dolce riso è stato mosso,
lunga fiata poi rimane oscura,
perché lo spirto non si rassicura.

That hostile form which in my body stands
Exulting without pause,
Which lords it in that room where will is spun,
    Self-smitten makes me long to reach those lands
Where I may find its cause,
For like seeks like and so has always done.
    Well do I know how snow goes to the sun
But can no more—I walk like him to my tomb
Who, at another's doom,
Goes on his lagging feet where life is taken.
As I draw near, I seem to hear someone
Call out, "Look at that man—he'll be dead soon."
I twist this way and that to see in whom
Mercy might live, but then her eyes awaken
From which I die unjustly and forsaken.

    What I've become, lord Love, so bruised each part,
You know, and I do not,
You who have stayed to see me under loam;
    And if my soul return into my heart,
Unfathomed and forgot
Is all I felt while it was far from home.
    As I arise and see the naked bone
Where one blow left me deaf and dumb and blind,
No comfort can I find
But shiver hard, fear deals such biting cold.
And by the pallor of my face is shown
What thunderbolt has fallen on my mind;
For though sweet smiles had loosed it (sweet but unkind),
Over my face long after darkness rolled,
Because my spirit found no certain hold.

Così m'hai concio, Amore, in mezzo l'alpi,
ne la valle del fiume
lungo il qual sempre sopra me se' forte:
    qui vivo e morto, come vuoi, mi palpi,
merzé del fiero lume
che sfolgorando fa via a la morte.
    Lasso, non donne qui, non genti accorte
veggio, a cui mi lamenti del mio male:
se a costei non ne cale,
non spero mai d'altrui aver soccorso.
E questa sbandeggiata di tua corte,
signor, non cura colpo di tuo strale:
fatto ha d'orgoglio al petto schermo tale,
ch'ogni saetta lì spunta suo corso;
per che l'armato cor da nulla è morso.

    O montanina mia canzon, tu vai:
forse vedrai Fiorenza, la mia terra,
che fuor di sé mi serra,
vota d'amore e nuda di pietate;
se dentro v'entri, va' dicendo: 'Omai
non vi può far lo mio fattor più guerra:
là ond'io vegno una catena il serra
tal, che se piega vostra crudeltate,
non ha di ritornar qui libertate'.

Thus have you scarred me, Love, where peak climbs peak
In that great river's sight
Along whose banks your shafts fall never short:
   You handle me alive, dead, as you seek,
Thanks to that double light
Which blazes death his path and sounds my mort.
   Alas, no man or lady of your true sort
Do I see here, to heed my want of bliss:
And if she's cold to this,
I cannot hope for aid from anyone.
But this fair outlaw from your noble court,
My lord, fears nothing where your arrows hiss:
Her pride is such a corselet that darts miss
Her breast, their mark, and fall with points undone—
Her armored heart thus feels the bite of none.

   O mountain song I sing, arise and go:
Maybe you'll come to Florence, my own land,
Which tells me I am banned,
Abyss to love and pity's wilderness;
If they should let you in, inform them, "NO
MORE can he attack who made me with his hand,
For whence I came such bonds hold him unmanned,
Though your old cruelty now should please you less,
He cannot come—he's mated at Love's chess."

NOTES

(What follows is largely a condensation of the rich materials provided in the commentary to the edition of the *Rime* by K. Foster and P. Boyde.)

1a–5:

The first five pair of sonnets in the collection all belong to the well-represented genre of formal poetic correspondence on conventional topics. It was usual to import into the reply at least one rhyme-sound from the sonnet to which one was responding. Years later, Dante returned to the genre (as in 72-75 or 84-88), but with far greater success than in these youthful exercises (to which my versions are if anything too kind). It should be noted that the attribution of these ten sonnets is usually the reverse of the attribution here.

2a: *"Whatever be your name, dear friend, your throw"*

Note that all the rhyme sounds of 2 are repeated.

3a: *"Nothing, dear friend, I find that here betrays"*

If the rhymes seem strained and the sense forced, then the effect of the original (which includes both *rime equivoche* and *rime composte*) has been captured.

5a: *"Love makes me love with such fidelity"*

l. 5: Dante da Maiano alludes to the sequel to Ovid's *Ars amatoria*, the *Remedia amoris*: the first work instructs us how to excite love; the second, how to escape it. Both were standard reading in the later Middle Ages.

7: *"When shepherd Love strikes hardest with his stave"*

An early experiment in "harsh rhymes" (cf. 77-80, 84-87), of uncertain date. Foster and Boyde believe it was written before

Dante's achievement of the *stil novo*; Barbi and Contini place it somewhat later.

l. 14: I am following Barbi-Maggini's interpretation of "a punto" here.

8–24:

The traditional dating of these poems is 1283-1288 (toward the end of the period which the *Vita nuova* commemorates). Foster and Boyde have revised the usual order to make it easier to see the three main kinds of poems represented: 1) double sonnets and one-stanza canzoni (8-12), in an improved version of the manner of 1-5; 2) sonnets written for and within a group of friends; 3) three poems written for a lady (or ladies) addressed as a flower (21-23).

8: *"If it's friend Lippo by whom I'm to be read"*

A double sonnet, 20 lines long, with six intercalated short lines.

ll. 13-20: Dante is requesting Lippo (perhaps the minor poet Lippo Pasci de' Bardi) either to set his poem (the naked girl) to music, or to get it set by someone else, or to "clothe" it in a poetic reply. In line 15, I follow Contini's reading, "a torto."

9: *"This my obedient heart"*

A "song of separation" and the first canzone-stanza in the collection. Note the unusual internal rhyme in l. 12.

13: *"My unrelenting mind, all retrospects"*

The first full-scale canzone—it may belong to a later period, and it is certainly a great advance in control and confidence over any of the preceding poems. Note the elaborate parade of argument.

ll. 20ff.: Since the image of the Lady is painted in Dante's sorrowing heart ("there," l. 22), she ought to prize it more highly, just as God does us because we are made in his image.

l. 48: I follow Barbi-Maggini's interpretation of "ond'io grande mi tegno."

14: *"Not now, no never now could they amend"*
An effective occasional poem securely dated to 1287 or earlier.

l. 3: The leaning tower Garisenda is a famous landmark in Bologna, where the skyline bristles with the stony keeps of a bellicose aristocracy. It seems that its beauty so absorbed Dante that he overlooked a still more beautiful woman, for which he here apologizes with comic effusiveness.

15: *"Guido, I wish that Lapo, you, and I"*
l. 1: Guido is Guido Cavalcanti, an outstanding poet and friend of Dante's. Lapo is Lapo Gianni de' Ricevuti, a notary and member of Dante's and Guido's circle of poets.

l. 3: The magic boat which figures especially in Arthurian legends.

l. 9: Guido's and Lapo's ladies, respectively.

l. 10: Dante's lady—perhaps Beatrice, perhaps one of the women with whom he screened his love for Beatrice (cf. *VN* 6-10). The arithmetical reference is to a list of the 60 most attractive Florentine women (*VN* 6), where Beatrice was number nine.

15a: *"If I were he whom love once called his clerk"*
l. 3: Cavalcanti refers to his former mistress Vanna (cf. 15, l. 9).

l. 8: Another lady, or perhaps Vanna still.

16: *"The brachets belling, the huntsman egging on"*
l. 8: The "one" is Dante's own guilty twinge of conscience.

19: *"My sonnet, if Meuccio's there to hear"*
A preface to a collection of verse ("brother sonnets") sent as a gift to (perhaps) the poet Meuccio Tolomei of Siena.

For direct address to the poem itself, cf. the close of several of Dante's canzoni (for instance, 13).

21: *"For a garland I"*
The first three lines of the *ballata* form its *ripresa* (cf. Introduction, Section ii).

l. 5: Women in Florence wore garlands frequently, and especially for the Mayday festival.

l. 12: Fioret may be the lady's name or a pseudonym (*"senhal"*).

l. 23: Either Dante has used a pre-existing melody (a common practice) or he is referring to the garland Fioret wore, out of which he has in effect woven this *ballata*.

22: *"My lady, dear, that mighty lord your eyes"*
A one-stanza canzone—the reference to "that tender flower" at line 15 connects it to numbers 21 and 23.

23: *"Ah Violet, in shade where Love reclines"*
A *ballata grande*, with a four-line *ripresa*, again on a "flower."

ll. 13f.: A reference to the imaginary hell reserved for *donne ingrate* who reject all lovers (cf. Andreas Capellanus' *De amore*, or Monteverdi's "Ballo delle ingrate").

25-32: Here Dante, very much under Cavalcanti's influence, gradually masters the "sweet new style."

25: *"That grievous love which brought me here tonight"*
l. 39: His soul will still be obsessed with the image of Beatrice.

32: *"Of self-compassion now I bear such weight"*
The distinctions made in this poem among soul, heart, and spirit, and between the lady and her image, are deliberate, precise, and consistent. Only Cavalcanti equaled Dante in this sort of scientific analysis of emotion, and that rarely.

240

l. 74: I.e., our human reason.

l. 79: "His fellows" = all the other human faculties.

38-39:

Like 36-37, which are included in the *VN*, these two sonnets were written on the occasion of Beatrice's grief for her father's death.

41: *"Mistress Dejection came to me one day"*

A presentiment of Beatrice's death.

l. 6: Dante reflects a common medieval prejudice about the citizens of Constantinople and its empire—"greco" even occurs as a noun meaning pride.

l. 10: I have substituted a cypress wreath, traditional in Western literature as a symbol of mourning, for the "hat" of the original, since the associations of the latter and its meaning would be misleading for us.

45: *"Ladies I saw who made a noble band"*

The heroine of this sonnet is almost certainly Beatrice.

58: *"By that same way which Beauty runs alone"*

This sonnet probably refers to the conflict in Dante's mind between Beatrice and the "gentle lady" of *VN* 35-38, and so would have been written in 1291/2. If not, it could be as late as 1302, the beginning of Dante's exile.

l. 5: The fortress of the will, guarded by the mind and soul, which consent or refuse to open it to the effects of the senses.

59: *"You through whose knowing moves the heavens' third sphere"*

Dante gives an extensive allegorical interpretation of this canzone in *Convivio* II, with the "other woman" acting as representative for his new love, philosophy. Of course, this does not exclude a literal reading in which the poem would describe a conflict between Dante's first love Beatrice and his passion for an actual woman, who is on the verge of victory at the poem's end. At some point between the *VN* and the *Commedia*, however, Dante unquestionably did transform Beatrice from a Florentine woman into a being who is a unity of both woman and Lady Philosophy. This canzone may well represent the moment when he made the crucial breakthrough into figural allegory by discovering Beatrice's true *total* meaning for himself.

l. 1: An apostrophe to the planetary intelligences that inhabit the heaven of Venus, which is literally the sphere of Love and allegorically the art or science of rhetoric. In the latter case, the intelligences would stand for past masters of rhetoric such as Cicero or Boethius, whose works had a particularly strong influence on Dante in the 1290s.

l. 3: It is a theme new to other men, inasmuch as it involves an opposition (as Foster and Boyde suggest) between the love of philosophy and the love of a woman who has been herself translated to a heavenly sphere.

ll. 10ff.: These lines encapsulate the subject matter of the rest of the poem. Allegorically, the "spirit" is the love of philosophy, transmitted by the "light" of philosophical texts.

ll. 14ff.: Since Beatrice's death, Dante's chief consolation has been the thought of her enjoying the bliss of heaven and the hope of soon joining her there. Now a new passion assaults him, promising a truer vision of paradise.

ll. 30ff.: Dante's soul laments the loss of its vision of Beatrice.

ll. 40ff.: The "spirit" of the first stanza reassures Dante in his confusion and fear. Note that she already claims him as her own ("dear soul of *ours*").

l. 52: A clear echo of Mary's words, Luke 1:38.

l. 53-55: This passage looks very much like a signal to the reader to look for an allegorical meaning behind the literal.

The surface of the poem, which is neither "hard" nor "intricate" in itself, could not account for such language.

l. 61: Again, Dante seems to be opposing the visible "beauty" of the poem to its inner significance. Average readers will have to content themselves with the former only.

60: *"Who talk of Love and know what you should say"*

Allegorically (cf. *Convivio* III.ix), this *ballata grande* records a stage of frustration along the way of philosophy.

ll. 17ff.: These lines speak allegorically of the delight of philosophy, and hence of philosophers, in their possession of wisdom, which takes the form of self-contemplation.

61: *"Love, who commands the chambers of my mind"*

In *Convivio* III, Dante explains this canzone as a panegyric to philosophy, whose soul is intellectual desire and whose body her total intelligible self, and in whose contemplation the poet delights (cf. *Purgatorio* II.106-117, where Casella is described as singing this very poem).

l. 1: Mind = reason, man's noblest faculty.

ll. 3-18: This theme of ideas beyond expression or even conception reaches its climax in the *Paradiso*.

l. 23: Intellect = the unfallen angels, who intuit wisdom in their intuition of God.

ll. 24-26: Earthly possession of love and wisdom can never fully satisfy lovers or philosophers.

l. 29: Perfect love or wisdom belongs to the transhuman level, and can only be conferred by God.

l. 45: The philosopher's actions express the beauty of his soul at all times.

ll. 51-54: By training us to accept apparent impossibilities as true, philosophy teaches us to accept as possible the miracles in which Christian dogma asks us to believe.

ll. 55ff.: Here we move from the beauty of the lady's "soul" (intellectual desire) to the beauty of her "body" (total

243

self), exemplified by her look and her smile. (The soul speaks most clearly through eyes and mouth.) The eyes = wisdom's proofs; the smile = its persuasions.

ll. 64-67: Note that wisdom produces *moral* excellence in the wise and destroys vices.

ll. 69-71: The proper lover is humble before his beloved; the Christian is humble before his weaknesses; the philosopher is humble before his limitations.

l 74: The "sister poem" is 60, here recanted.

62: *"My words that people speak of far and near"*

This sonnet records a phase of revulsion against the study of philosophy and perhaps the use of allegory in verse as well (cf. the literal statement of 69 and 70).

l. 1: "Words" = Dante's poems.

l. 3: "Her" = the new lady.

l. 8: In this palinode, Dante says he has written his last poem to unattainable philosophy.

l. 11: "Older sisters" = either numbers 25-32 (in a period of unhappy love) or 47-50 and 55-57 (on Beatrice's death).

63: *"O tender rhymes who talk both far and near"*

Dante repudiates the preceding poem, hoping that this sonnet and his earlier "tender rhymes" will intercede for him.

l. 6: "That lord" = Love.

64–66:

The style and youthful heroine (*giovinetta* or *pargoletta*) of these three lyrics marks them out as a coherent group. They may refer to a literal affair after Beatrice's death (cf. *Purgatorio* XXXI.58-60), but they can also be read as allegories (cf. 61 to 64, and 60 to 65-66).

64: *"Young is my beauty, early yet and new"*

The originality of this *ballata mezzana* is that the lady praises herself.

ll. 15-18: Again the theme of a beauty or wisdom which no one still on earth can fully grasp.

l. 23: "One" = Love, as usual.

66: *"And who will ever look without great fear"*

ll. 13ff.: The "power" is death; it was believed that a pearl became a pearl by absorbing good influences from a star.

67: *"Love, you whose power comes from heaven's hold"*

l. 1: Literally, the "influence" from the heaven of Venus (cf. 61); allegorically, God's goodness, especially as it excites the desire for wisdom in men (the sun is a common medieval symbol for God).

l. 27: The water acts as a lens to focus the sunlight.

ll. 28-30: Note the series of modes of vision that culminates here: direct, then refracted, then reflected (in the latter, the sun goes to her eyes to his eyes and back to her eyes).

ll. 42-45: After much deliberation, I have chosen to follow Foster and Boyde's interpretation of this recondite passage rather than Contini's. Earthly flames act as "tokens" of the sun's "virtue," with which they are consubstantial but which they neither increase nor decrease by their operations. The analogy that comes to mind is the relationship of word and concept (or *signifiant* and *signifié*)—the former diffuses knowledge of the latter without affecting it in any physical sense.

l. 60: "Peace" refers on one plane to sexual fulfillment, on another, to the temporary vision of truth a philosopher can sometimes attain on earth.

68: *"I find the might of Love so burdensome"*

In certain stylistic features and in its structure, this allegorical canzone, written perhaps ca. 1295, harks back to the manner and period of poems 25-32. Dante's development follows no simple straight line; instead, certain poems show him doubling back on himself to recover elements that he had discarded but that had a place in the ultimate synthesis.

ll. 24-27: By turning away from him, the lady no longer can see his love and his desire to serve; in addition, the value of her lover-servant, as he sees it, decreases insofar as he is unable to serve her; thus, she is doubly the loser.

l. 32: Allegorically, Dante is speaking of spiritual or "second" death, the consequence of ceasing to love wisdom.

ll. 46-48: Dante refers to his immaturity in the pursuit of philosophy—her "youth" is a reflection of his.

ll. 92-94: The sense of the Italian is uncertain here. Foster and Boyde interpret it as a warning against hypocrites who hide their evil by consorting with the good, and I follow suit.

l. 99: The "third one" may be Guido Cavalcanti, from whom Dante was for a while estranged.

ll. 103-106: No editor has completely explained the sense of these lines. My translation is simply a slash at the Gordian knot.

69: *"Those words of love which only yesterday"*

This and the next canzone are striking experiments in explicitly didactic poetry, aimed not at elite readers but at all those willing to hear. The allegorical poems leading up to them (59-68) deal with topics beyond the sphere of the love-lyric, but they maintain the *stil novo* Dante had mastered while working in that sphere. Now he sheds that style and enters on a new phase of growth, inclusive rather than exclusive, reaching out constantly for new ways of expression. (See *Convivio* IV for Dante's commentary.)

l. 8: Both "tender" manner and allegorical mode are rejected here.

l. 18: The "sovereign" is truth.

l. 20: Again Dante speaks of the philosopher's rapt contemplation of the fact of his own contemplation of wisdom.

l. 21: Frederick II (1194-1250), after Aristotle, as Dante later discovered.

ll. 38-40: Dante has equally harsh words elsewhere for degenerate aristocrats. The last line reflects the belief that insofar as one ceases to live by reason, one is already dead.

ll. 41-43: Man is not a tree, nor is he simply "animate" either—he is "rational" as well.

ll. 52ff.: No one can paint an image unless he first conceives it in his mind—in a sense, becomes the image he renders.

ll. 85-87: *Nicomachean Ethics* ii. 6. 1107ª I.

ll. 91ff.: Nobility underlies and comprehends all the virtues —in Kenneth Burke's nomenclature, it acts as a "God-term."

ll. 105-108: Shamefastness is a sign of nobility yet is not considered to be a moral virtue. Therefore, nobility comprises the virtues and other "goods" as well.

l. 109: Virtue is a mixture of nobility and passion, with nobility predominant, just as "sloe" is a combination of black and purple, with the black predominant. (For Dante, nobility is primarily a high degree of rationality.)

ll. 114-115: The noblest men approach the level of the angels.

l. 141: Dante names this poem after Aquinas' *Contra Gentiles*.

l. 143: "Our lady" = philosophy, who lives in all who are wise or who love wisdom.

l. 146: "Your friend" = nobility.

70: *"Now that lord Love has quite abandoned me"*
The principal concept of this poem, *leggiadria* (its root is Latin *levis*, "light in weight"), has no exact English equivalent. It includes such notions as "charm," "elegance," "gaiety," "buoyancy," but could also mean "frivolity" or "falseness." I have translated it as "gallantry," hoping to suggest its ambiguity and that it belongs to an ethical code of love-relationships which has today dwindled to polite convention but was an admired ideal in Dante's time.

The style is rugged and aggressive, and Dante has lent it a special air of irascible impatience by the use of rapid-fire internal rhymes (see ll. 1-3 and 7-9 of each stanza).

ll. 4-6: Love has courteously released Dante, for the moment, from his frustrating pursuit of wisdom, and he seizes the opportunity for writing of a value which is outstanding for the courtesy it produces.

l. 10: "Vile" = non-courtly, therefore without *leggiadria*.

l. 17-19: An effective defense of *leggiadria* will in fact prove Dante capable of continuing to follow the way of philosophy.

ll. 55-57: "It isn't women who are leading otherwise 'courtois' men astray."

ll. 58-60: "The stars have decreed a decline in gallantry, even worse than I have described."

ll. 62ff.: Primarily Beatrice, but philosophy as well.

ll. 74ff.: This is the crux of Dante's argument. He has to concede that *leggiadria* (unlike nobility) is not appropriate to all walks of life. Indeed, scholars and the clergy in their "hall" properly identify it as "mixed," i.e., partly virtue, but partly no more than socially desirable qualities. But Dante, who is implicitly upholding the claims of the active life to be recognized as a valid alternative to the contemplative, follows his concession with a splendid picture of the excellences of *leggiadria*, equating it to that God-symbol, the sun. Emotionally, if not logically, he thereby wins his case.

ll. 112-114: That is, gallantry, which is like the sun.

l. 133: Note that there is no *congedo*. As Dante says at line 69, he doesn't know who will listen to this poem and therefore he has no address to send it to.

71: *"Talking of love and failing to agree"*

Dante states and reconciles the two principles of his life: *fin'amor* and moral philosophy. Note that both converge in Love. Their discussion centers on a traditional courtly *quaestio*: can one love two people at once? Ultimately, Dante solved the problem by discovering that both were Beatrice.

l. 12: That is, Love.

72-74a:

For Dante, these sonnets revive his youthful habit of poetic exchange but now in the form of a highly literary "flyting" rather than mannerly ratiocination on matters of *fin'amor*. They were probably written sometime between 1293 and 1296, perhaps before poems 59-71, but since they mark yet another stage in Dante's growth, annexation of the "low," comic style crucial later on in the *Inferno*, Foster and Boyde place them here before the *petrose*, which blend high and low in a revolutionary way.

72: *"Whoever heard her coughing, the poor dear"*
l. 2: "Bicci" seems to have been the nickname of Forese Donati (d. 1296).

l. 4: Cf. note to number 79, ll. 25-27.

l. 8: That is, Bicci isn't doing his duty as a husband.

l. 11: Physicians believed that women needed sex to stay healthy—a pleasant doctrine.

72a: *"All night I coughed and coughed—you see"*
ll. 9-10: It is unclear just why Dante's father is in bondage. Perhaps he had died as a usurer, perhaps his son had as yet failed to avenge a wrong he had endured (cf. 74a, ll. 1-4).

l. 11: God's grace came from the East, it was thought, and so would Christ at the Last Day.

73: *"You'll have a knot of Solomon in your gut"*
Dante turns the notion of a "knot" against Forese and lashes him for gluttony, the root of his indigence and larceny. The unfortunate man turns up on the sixth level of the *Purgatorio* starving away his past sins.

l. 4: Debts were recorded on parchment and if unpaid could land you in prison. Thus, in the end the lamb evens the score.

ll. 7ff.: You may reform now, but you've already eaten your way into ruin and a cell.

73a: *"Go reimburse San Gal before you cast"*

l. 1: San Gal was a spital on the Bologna road outside the walls.

l. 7: Forese alleges that Dante had also gone begging to Castello Altrafonte, near the Ponte Vecchio.

l. 10: Dante's stepsister and stepbrother, respectively.

l. 11: A workhouse near S. Pier Maggiore, under the patronage of Donati.

74: *"Bicci my boy, you son of God-knows-who"*

ll. 13ff.: The Italian is obscure, and the innuendo uncertain.

74a: *"Oh, you were Alighieri's son, I'd say"*

ll. 1-4: Most of this is highly ironical. A true son would have avenged the swindling of his father, as Dante has not; ergo, Dante is probably a bastard. Dante senior was dead by 1283, which means that at least a decade of inaction had elapsed—the other day, indeed!

ll. 13ff.: The Italian refers to the practice of toting up accounts with the help of millet seeds. Barbi suggests a different interpretation than the one followed here: "It's time to end this game (the exchange of sonnets) and add up the score."

75a–75:

This exchange is quite in the old manner and on a traditional love-topic—note that Dante repeats all the rhyme-sounds of the first sonnet in his reply. Editors believe it to postdate the *leggiadria* canzone, however (cf. 75a, ll. 13).

75: *"Dante to you, who called upon his name"*

ll. 9-11: The original is far from clear. Most editors take line 9 to mean that the woman is unmarried, and I follow suit.

76: *"Master Brunetto, this little maid was led"*

This sonnet claims to preface another poem, sent as a gift (cf. 8), but mocks the recipient for his lowbrow hedonism.

l. 14: Giano ("Zany") is unidentified—he may have been a half-wit or he may have been the formidable author of the second part of the *Romance of the Rose*, whose explanations are far more difficult than the questions they purport to answer—Jean de Meung.

77: *"Heaven's wheel my scaffold has brought me to that place"*

This is the first of four remarkable poems on "Petra," or "stone" (see Introduction). Here the lover is the landscape; in the next poem, a sestina, the beloved is.

ll. 1-6: In these lines, Dante transforms the seasonal opening conventional in medieval love-lyric into a "scientific" astrological comment on the speaker's state of soul. Cold Saturn is at the height of his power, Venus at her nadir, in conjunction and hidden by the sun, and Dante's birth-sign at its aphelion, where it is almost impotent (cf. the helplessness the speaker describes). Taking this passage as his point of departure, Philip Damon interprets the poem as a symbolic portrait of the failure of love (cf. "the evening star"), prudence, and the contemplative faculty leading to spiritual petrifaction and fears of Judgment (cf. the "spring" of the *congedo*). (See *University of California Publications in Classical Philology* 15.6, 1961, "Modes of Analogy in Ancient and Medieval Verse," chap. six.) The passage also acts as a periphrasis for a date of December 1296 (cf. Dante's usual practice in the Commedia), which has important though ambiguous implications for the chronology of the *Rime*.

l. 1: Concerning "my scaffold," see the Introduction.

l. 7-9: A planet rising in the sign of Cancer at midwinter will stand higher in the heavens than at any other time of year; thus, it will cast its shortest shadow (cf. the sun at the summer solstice, when *it* is in Cancer).

ll. 14-16: Dante ignores the *scirocco*'s warmth and emphasizes its humidity and strength (the "no other" of l. 18 refers to its opponent, the north wind). Norman Douglas' *South Wind* portrays vividly the overcast and oppression of spirits that accompany it. I render "Etiopia" as "Egyptian"—modern readers do not associate Ethiopia with sand, though in fact the country does include much low desert. "Peregrin" has been translated as "alien," which is the sense that I believe appropriate here. To translate it as "pilgrim" would be misleading, especially for readers aware of Dante's quite different use of "peregrino" in the *Comedy*. Here, the English word would suggest a humble, peaceable old gentleman with staff and scrip, which is quite wrong for Dante's *scirocco*!

ll. 23-25: I have preferred to picture Love as a fisherman rather than as a fowler—the Italian *ragne* refers to "webs" or "nets."

l. 29: The unsetting constellation of the Great Bear.

l. 41: In spring, the sun enters Aries, the Ram (cf. the opening of *The Canterbury Tales*).

ll. 54-55: Traditional learning held that vapors in the earth could produce floods, winds, even earthquakes (cf. *Inferno* III.132 or *Purgatorio* XXVIII.97-9).

l. 69: "The Seven" = *questi geli* ("these frosts") in the Italian. I here refer to the "stars of ice" of line 29 and the position of the seven planets in the first stanza.

78: *"To dwindling day and the great ring of shadow"*

The form of this poem is taken from Arnaut Daniel's sestina "Lo ferm voler" (see Hamlin, Ricketts, Hathaway, *Introduction à l'étude de l'ancien provençal*, Geneva, 1967, pp. 198-200). Dante discusses its operation in *DVE* II.xiii.2. There are six key words used to end the lines, and the order of their recurrence in each stanza is fixed by a principle of retrogression (the first line of a stanza ends with the same word as the last line of the preceding stanza, etc.). Each key word occupies all possible positions by the end of the sixth and final stanza, and the speaker seems to contemplate obsessively and motionlessly the inner surfaces of a cube of stone. There is no issue, only the incantatory repetition of their six names (shadow, hills, grass, green, rock, woman) and, in the *congedo*, the final contraction toward a point—the next step would be the elimination of all other words, or the silence which ends all poems but seems the necessary conclusion of this sestina's logic. For successful examples of the form in English, see Sidney, Pound, Auden, and Eliot.

l. 1: This poem too begins in winter (cf. the "ring" to the "wheel" of 77).

ll. 19-20: These lines refer to the magical "virtue" of precious stones (as in medieval lapidaries) and to magical wounds such as one finds in Arthurian tales (as with the Grail King).

ll. 27-30: Dante evokes the *hortus conclusus*, the traditional "enclosed garden" of secular and sacred medieval lore (cf. Song of Songs 4.12 and the loving parody of the motif at the end of Chaucer's *Merchant's Tale*).

l. 31: This may refer to the shadowy leaf-time of summer, the long shadows of evening, or the darkness of winter. As Foster and Boyde note, the last interpretation has the advantage of returning us to the poem's opening.

79: *"You, Love, you must see clearly how this woman"*

Foster and Boyde suggest that this poem be called a "canzonesestina" rather than a "double sestina." The stanza is twice the length of the sestina's, but there are five key- or rhyme-words, not six, and their arrangement is far simpler—"the last rhyme-word of a stanza becomes the first of the next and the rest all move down one place" (*F & B*, vol. 2, p. 269). The stanzas themselves are divided into two major sections, each of which is further subdivided—this contrasts sharply with the monolithic stanzas of 78 and reflects the structure usual in the canzone (as in 80). Dante here loads himself down with chains, and critics have looked askance at the result. For a demurral and defense, see the Introduction. Here I will add only that Dante has taken the conventional themes of the medieval love-lyric and infused them with a hallucinatory intensity beside which contemporary French *chansons d'amour* and German *minnesang* pale.

ll. 25-30: It was thought that quartz was produced by extreme frost, a notion earlier poets had often made capital of.

ll. 49-50: The "Power" is Love, seen in the grandest available terms (cf. *Purgatorio* XVII.91-93).

ll. 65-66: *"La novità che per tua forma luce"* certainly refers

to the form of the poem (cf. *DVE* II.xiii), and I have tried
to bring this out in my translation.

80: *"Now would I file my speech into a rasp"*

This, the last and greatest of the four *rime petrose*, has a
propulsive movement the others, in their examination of a
single state of mind from all sides, unquestionably lack. In
the first line, Dante alerts us to its experimental aspect, the
consistent use of harsh sounds, especially in rhyme position,
and I have tried to suggest the effect of the original in the
rhymes of the first few lines. It was impossible to sustain the
effect consistently however, without serious cost to the rhythm
and sense; hence, most of the rhymes thereafter are of only
average difficulty.

l. 5: The jasper, it was thought, was able to protect *chaste*
wearers against harm.

ll. 33-34: The syntax of these lines in the Italian is ambigu-
ous. I follow Foster and Boyde, though with less than a whole
heart.

l. 36: Dido commits suicide in Book IV of the *Aeneid*,
abandoned by its hero, Venus' son and Cupid's half-brother.
The Middle Ages saw in her a case of illicit carnal love.

81: *"Around my heart, as if they went to earth"*

A great lyric meditation (written probably in 1304 or later)
on Dante's exile and the exile of justice from earth (see also
Paradiso XVII).

l. 35: Justice is Astraea, sister to Venus, who is Love's moth-
er. Here she is an exile on earth, rather than the last celestial
who left it, as in Ovid.

l. 46: The source of the Nile was believed to have lain
within the Earthly Paradise.

ll. 47ff.: I read the original as referring to the near-per-
pendicular rays of the equatorial sun.

ll. 50-54: The genealogy is as follows: justice (divine and
natural law) gives birth to the law of nations (*ius gentium*)

which in turn bears the written law of legislation proper. Each birth occurs through an act of self-contemplation at the level of reason, with God's wisdom as the mirror.

ll. 65ff.: Men suffer from the exile of justice and love, not the qualities of justice and love themselves, which dwell in the world of eternity. The suggestion of determinism in l. 68 accords with 70, ll. 58-60 but not with Dante's views on free will in the *Commedia*.

ll. 77-80: The primary reference is probably *not* to the defeat of the Florentine Whites by the Blacks, since at the poem's end Dante is seeking reconciliation with the victors, not the noble death alongside the losers of which l. 80 speaks; rather, it is to a victory of evil in general and to Dante's resolve to stand with the "good" even if he dies for it (see Contini's note).

ll. 81-84: If Dante could only return to Florence, he would bear all else.

ll. 88-90: Dante says that he has repented his "fault" and should therefore be forgiven. In view of ll. 102-107, the fault was probably an earlier political action directed against the Blacks.

ll. 91ff.: Cf. the end of 59 for this opposition between external beauty and hidden inner meaning. "What lies outside" includes the literal sense as well as form and style in this case.

ll. 101-102: Dante declares his neutrality—he is of neither faction.

l. 103: He must flee because he is under sentence of death in Florence.

l. 104: The Blacks could pardon Dante, if they chose.

ll. 106-107: Dante asks for amnesty of operations conducted by him as one of the Whites since his exile in 1302.

82: *"If you have seen my eyes desiring tears"*
l. 3: Justice.
l. 4: I follow Contini's interpretation here.

ll. 6-7: The murderer is probably Pope Clement V; the tyrant, Philip the Fair of France, who had the Pope in his pocket.

l. 12: Justice again.

83: *"Emboldening pain has set my heart on fire"*

Another great ethical canzone, written after 1302 and before 1305, and probably intended for inclusion and interpretation in the *Convivio*. Its associative metaphors, stylistic range, and angry passion suggest the poetic world of the *Comedy*.

ll. 12ff.: Dante takes the traditional line that rational virtue is proper to men, beauty to women. Love enables the two to achieve union in marriage. But if men have lost all virtue, women should withhold their love and conceal their beauty, since the union God intended is now impossible.

l. 21: Dante may be suggesting actual self-defacement here —if thine eye offend thee, pluck it out.

l. 33: The "lady" is probably the human soul, virtue's "mistress," but she may be divine wisdom instead.

ll. 41ff.: The love of wisdom sets us free from all transient things and makes us lords over our own souls.

ll. 57-58: Dante must gear down his language so that the ladies can follow him (cf. the supposed audience of the first stanza).

ll. 62ff.: Avoid the evil lest you become like them or reveal that you are one of them.

l. 81: A dog can live on bread alone, but not a man.

ll. 93-94: Evil influences from the stars hem us in and foster vice.

ll. 99-105: The miserly go clothed while the virtuous go naked—hence the misers are harmful both to themselves and to others, who deserve but do not receive their charity.

ll. 106ff.: Virtue is a falconer, the miser her ill-tempered subject, the bait the divine beauty she manifests.

ll. 133ff.: Leaves of love can elicit good from a good root

—but all such leaves have withered. Therefore, the proper course is to deny any response to the men of today, whether the lady is wholly or only partly good, and thus avoid falling to the level of the beasts.

ll. 150-153: The countess to whom Dante refers is not securely identified. *Bianca* = white = beautiful or wise; *giovanna* = young = wise or "courtois"; *(con)tessa* = countess = "courtois" or beautiful. She serves as the paradigm for the virtue and conduct Dante has been urging on his audience.

84-88:

This sonnet-exchange with Cino da Pistoia (d. 1336), a fine poet and close younger friend of Dante's, can for the most part be dated to the period of exile. Numbers 84a-84 were probably written earlier, but 85-85a could but need not have been. Whatever the dating, it seems best to present all ten poems together as a group. Dante displays extraordinary virtuosity in his rhymes, especially where he is constrained to follow Cino's, and the metaphorical density as a consequence is exceptionally high. It is instructive to contrast his mastery in these sonnets to his first attempts at the form and manner fifteen or more years before (1-5).

84a: *"Just now, Love swore that if I'd fix"*

l. 1: Cino had long suffered an unhappy passion for a "dark lady" (see his earlier sonnets).

l. 4: "Beatrix" = a woman who gives bliss.

l. 14: Another reference to the "dark lady."

84: *"I've seen the thing before, five times or six"*

l. 3: The Sun, whose child Phaethon fell into the Po, causes the rootless wood to bear leaves.

l. 7: Under the circumstances, any fruit would be false or worthless, since the earth (or, in another interpretation, the native sap) did not produce it.

l. 9: "Green" has complex implications: youth, fickleness,

unripeness. It may even allude to the color worn by the enchantress Ninue, who deluded and destroyed the wizard Merlin (cf. l. 12).

85: *"I find none here who'll reason properly"*
l. 2: Love.

ll. 7ff.: This sounds very much like a reference to the discomforts of exile (cf. 89.67ff.), as well as to Luke ii.7 and ix.58 (cf. 85a-7ff.).

l. 12: "Messer" is the specific title for jurists.

86a: *"Dante, if by some chance it feels the wane"*
ll. 1-8: A lover who survives the death of his love has the right to transfer his love elsewhere. "The two extremes" are birth and death, or "cold" and "heat," or the fates. (Cino is trying very hard to talk like Dante.)

l. 12: Both the eyes of the new woman and the Black and White factions that troubled Pistoia as well as Dante.

86: *"I have stood now in the brightness of Love's beams"*
ll. 1ff.: Dante refers to his passion for Beatrice, treated here as not merely spiritual.

ll. 7ff.: The collision of dry and wet vapors supposedly produced thunder.

ll. 9-14: Neither will nor wisdom avail against passion. We must go wherever he drives us. (Contrast *Purgatorio* XVIII. 40-74, where Dante seems to recant the doctrine of this sonnet.)

87a: *"Seeking an ore in Love's profoundest mine"*
l. 3: Cino refers to the recipient of his sonnet, Moroello Malaspina, whose name means "Bad Thorn." Dante stayed at Malaspina's in 1306/7 and may have been asked by his host to write a reply to Cino at that time.

ll. 12-14: Cino wishes Love would soften his mistress' stony heart, just as God let Moses make water spring from the living rock (Exodus xvii.6).

87: *"That your sweet voice could only be a sign"*

ll. 7ff.: The "gold" of the capacity for love, of which one traditional symptom was a marked pallor.

88: *"I thought that I was through with all the store"*

ll. 1-4: Dante is saying that he thought he had left love-poetry and the *stil novo* behind for good and would now concentrate on philosophy—or perhaps the *Comedy*.

88a: *"Driven, Dante, from native roof and door"*

ll. 9-11: Although his first and only lady has been ruthless toward him, Cino has not given up and turned elsewhere.

89: *"Love, against whom I must speak my sorrow's fill"*

This valedictory canzone, usually dated to 1307/8, returns to the style Dante had perfected before the moral canzoni or the *rime petrose* but communicates a degree of passion unknown to that earlier style.

l. 33: Love has stripped Dante of his free will.

ll. 34-36: Dante is forced to seek for the actual woman to whom the mental image corresponds.

l. 37: To rise to the sun, snow must of course melt away and so "die."

ll. 38ff.: The death by execution Dante describes here is probably a form of spiritual death, either damnation or the loss of reason (see the following stanza).

ll. 43-45: Unluckily for him, his desperate gaze is caught by his lady's, which is lethal to him.

ll. 49ff.: Dante's language suggests an inversion of the mystic experience, reason lost rather than transcended.

l. 62: The upper Arno valley, in the Apennines, the locale of Dante's passion (cf. the *petrose*).

ll. 72-74: cf. Number 80, ll. 3-8.

SELECTED BIBLIOGRAPHY

Editions of the *Rime*:

Le Rime, ed. D. Mattalia, Turin, 1943.
Rime, ed. G. Contini, Turin, 1946, 2nd ed.; repr. 1965.
Rime della "Vita Nuova" e della giovinezza, ed. M. Barbi and
    F. Maggini, Florence, 1956.
Dante's Lyric Poetry, ed. K. Foster and P. Boyde, Oxford,
    1967. The place from which to start further investigations.
Rime della maturità e dell'esilio, ed. M. Barbi and V. Perni-
    cone, Florence, 1969.

Verse Translations:

Charles Lyell, *The Canzoniere of Dante Alighieri*, London,
    1835.
D. G. Rossetti, *Dante and His Circle*, London, 1874. Highly
    selective, but poetically the best yet available.
E. H. Plumptre, *Commedia and canzoniere*, London, 1886.
L. de' Lucchi, *Minor Poems*, London, 1926. A weak perform-
    ance, but the only other twentieth-century verse transla-
    tion of the collection as a whole of which I am aware.
H. S. Vere-Hodge, *Odes*, Oxford, 1963. This rendering of the
    canzoni and sestinas is of scholarly value, particularly for
    its commentary, but it is unsuccessful as English verse.

Secondary Literature:

Patrick Boyde, *Dante's Style in his Lyric Poetry*, Cambridge, 1971. This meticulous stylistic study is the fullest treatment of the *Rime* available in English. Its select bibliography, on pp. 332-347, and the bibliography given at the end of the Foster-Boyde edition, volume II, pp. 363-371, offer excellent guidance to the rest of the considerable literature.

INDEX OF FIRST LINES

THE LOCKERT LIBRARY OF POETRY IN TRANSLATION

LIBRARY OF CONGRESS CATALOGING IN PUBLICATION DATA

Dante Alighieri, 1265-1321.
  Dante's Rime.

  (The Lockert library of poetry in translation)
  Bibliography: p.
  Includes index.
  I. Diehl, Patrick.
PQ4315.52.D5   851'.1   79-83984
ISBN 0-691-06409-1
ISBN 0-691-01361-6 pbk.